END TIME
PROPHECY
Made Simple

END TIME
PROPHECY
Made Simple

ELWOOD TROST

XULON PRESS

Xulon Press
2301 Lucien Way #415
Maitland, FL 32751
407.339.4217
www.xulonpress.com

Printed in the United States of America.

ISBN-13: 9781545615607

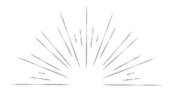

Blessed is the man who trusts in the Lord, and whose HOPE is the Lord. For he shall be like a tree planted by the waters, which spreads out its roots by the river, and will not fear when heat comes; but its leaf will be green, and will not be anxious in the year of drought, nor will cease from yielding fruit (Jeremiah 17:7-8).

Rejoicing in HOPE, patient in tribulation, continuing steadfastly in prayer (Romans 12:12).

See that you do not refuse Him who speaks. For if they did not escape who refused Him who spoke on earth, much more shall we not escape if we turn away from Him who speaks from heaven, whose voice then shook the earth; but now He has promised, saying, "Yet once more I shake not only the earth, but also heaven." Now this, "Yet once more," indicates the removal of those things that are being shaken, as of things that are made, that the things which cannot be shaken may remain. Therefore, since we are receiving a kingdom which cannot be shaken, let us have grace, by which we may serve God acceptably with reverence and godly fear. For our God is a consuming fire (Hebrews 12:25-29).

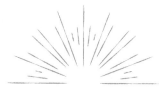

A NOTE TO THE READER

JESUS' SECOND COMING IS NEAR AND WHEN He returns things get better for the next 1,000 years. Hallelujah, but the road from now until Jesus returns will be a difficult time.

If you ask for the Holy Spirit's guidance as you read the Bible for yourself you will be able to understand the Scripture about the end-times. God has given us approximately 150 chapters in the Bible about the second coming of Christ, and Jesus told us, "To watch."

We shouldn't believe something just because it is popular, but we should take the time and check it out ourselves with God's word. The Bereans took everything Paul the apostle was teaching and checked it out with the Scriptures to see if it was true (Acts 17:11).

Daniel received a prophecy about the end-times and the book of Daniel has been sealed until the time of the end (Daniel 12:4-9). Today it is being opened up to give us more understanding of what God is doing today.

My prayer is that this book is a blessing to you and helps you understand the end-times and what is required of us as believers as we see that day approaching.

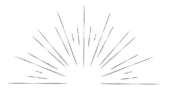

TABLE OF CONTENTS

DEDICATION

THIS BOOK IS DEDICATED TO GOD, THE FATHER, Who is good and full of love; Jesus Christ, His Son, who gave His life for us, so we could have life. He stepped down from His throne into darkness, and took on Satan the god of this age, and defeated him. He is returning soon to take back the earth from the enemy of our soul. Also, I dedicate this book to the Holy Spirit who is moving today to bring order out of chaos by giving gifts and releasing power to the people of God and bringing unity to God's people.

Not forgetting God's people who are waking up from their deep sleep and following Jesus into the battle of redemption. Together these four are an awesome and fearful sight to the soon coming Antichrist.

Endorsements

"As the Lord's return draws near, He is raising up voices; calling upon His people to awaken out of our slumber because our salvation is now nearer than when we first believed. As John the Baptist did before the Lord's first coming, they are calling upon the people of God to repent. Also, preparing the way in their hearts, because once again the kingdom of God is close at hand. Elwood Trost is one of these voices. It is high time that the Church should awaken and prepare herself as the espoused Bride of Christ. It is imperative that the Church recognize the hour in which she finds herself and begins to sharpen her focus on end-time events - putting to the test commonly held beliefs. We can no longer afford ourselves the luxury of saying, 'it will all pan out in the end.' I am grateful to Elwood for being obedient to his call and making his voice heard as he does in this book."
George Sidney Hurd
Missionary and Author; Mitu, Colombia

"The most powerful, paradigm changing books ever written have gone against the flow and dramatically redirected the current of prevailing beliefs. This book by Elwood Trost is such a book. The Lord's armies currently in America have been lulled to sleep by resting in the belief that they will escape by 'rapture' the difficult days ahead. This book will wake them up, eradicate the flight response and initiate intercession for what is coming to planet Earth!"

Bill Sawyer

Founder & CEO
www.BusinessNetworkinginChrist.com;

"Which is it? Pre-Trib rapture? Mid -Trib rapture? Pre-Wrath rapture? Or Post-Trib rapture? *End Time Prophecy Made Simple* gives a good explanation into all the rapture theories and excellent insight in what the Bible has to say about the last days. Elwood Trost has done his home-work!"
Deb Feist, Author; Listening Prayer:
How to Hear the Voice of God

FOREWORD

HAVING GROWN UP STUDYING THE SCOFIELD Reference Bible, reading Hal Lindsey's *The Late Great Planet Earth* and listening to Larry Norman's song, "*I Wish We'd All Been Ready*," I was a dyed in the wool Pre-Tribulation rapturist. When the Lord got a hold of my life as a young man, I began to devour the word. It was then that I discovered I John 2:27, "But the anointing which you have received from Him abides in you, and you do not need that anyone teach you..." I would let the Holy Spirit be my teacher. In my pursuit of becoming a teacher of the word, I availed myself of every tool I could lay hold of to give myself completely to an 'in depth' study of the Bible including the original languages and Church history. Equipped with that knowledge, I began to realize that much of what was being taught in popular Christianity was simply a rehashed version of someone else's systematic theology. I began to rely very heavily on the words of Jesus that state, "If anyone wills to do His will, he shall know concerning the doctrine, whether it is from God..." (John 7:17). That has been my herme-neutic: my approach to interpretation. He has been faithful to teach and guide me. He has answered every question I have ever had about doctrine. It was under the teaching ministry of Kingdom of the Cults author, the late Walter Martin, that I first was exposed to a Scriptural challenge debunking the Pre-Trib rapture.

He used Revelation 20 to show that the first resurrection (i.e., "the rapture"), included the great tribulation saints. That was all I needed. A faithful search of all the texts revealed that each one presented the same scenario: the tribulation, Christ's coming and then the resurrection or the rapture. There no longer seemed to be any Scriptural support for a secret, separate, and imminent rapture. It was then that I read, *The Blessed Hope* by George Eldon Ladd. He carefully chronicles the development and dissemination of the doctrine of the Pre-Trib rapture and its beginnings just over a century ago.

Unfortunately, almost every popular radio and television preacher teaches this doctrine. The effort made to defend it amazes me, yet I remain unconvinced and all the more determined to see this false doctrine exposed. I am thankful to my friend Elwood Trost, who has been on a similar journey. He has done a great job with a simple explanation of the second coming. You will find his treatment very readable and packed with insights. Enjoy the journey...

Greg Escher, pastor;
Grace Community Church
Fort Bragg, California

PREFACE

IN 1973 I WAS WATCHING A TELEVISION PRO-
gram on Matthew chapter 24 about the signs of the second coming
of Christ. It caught my interest because I wasn't a believer at the
time and I realized I wasn't ready for Jesus to come back. So I quit
my job and moved to a log cabin in Northern California overlooking
the Pacific Ocean. I didn't realize it at the time, but God was calling
me into His kingdom.

I began reading the Bible and read where you needed to be born-
again to see the kingdom of God (John 3:3). So I asked to be born-
again and to my surprise God's Spirit came down on me like a
mighty wind just like it is recorded in the book of Acts.

*Then Peter said to them, "Repent, and let every one of you be
baptized in the name of Jesus Christ for the remission of sins; and
you shall receive the gift of the Holy Spirit. For the promise is to
you and to your children, and to all who are afar off, as many as the
Lord our God will call" (Acts 2:38-39).*

The Holy Spirit began to reveal and help me understand end-
time prophecy. Then, I began to realize that a lot of what was being
taught about the second coming of Christ was not what was being
revealed to me and a lot of it was *not* Scriptural either.

We have the Scriptures so how could this be happening? Satan
was able to deceive people during the first coming of Christ and they
had the Scriptures; why shouldn't he keep on trying? Satan knows if

he can confuse people about the second coming of Christ they will be a target to fall away during the tribulation, and Jesus tells us that this is exactly what will happen:

Then they will deliver you up to tribulation and kill you, and you will be hated by all nations for My name's sake. And then many will be offended, will betray one another, and will hate one another (Matthew 24:9-10).

I believe God has called me to warn the body of Christ for what we are about to experience. In the book of Ezekiel God says if you see the sword coming and you don't warn the people you will be held responsible for their deaths (Ezekiel 33:3-6). My purpose for writing this book is to use the Bible to show Christians the truth that we are *not* going to escape the tribulation like many have been taught and most of the popular media believes and supports.

The rain falls on the just and unjust. The tribulation is not God punishing His people, because Jesus took our punishment on Himself, but God will use the tribulation to prepare a bride for His Son (Revelation 19:7). He will use it to separate the wheat from the tares that have been growing together (Matthew 13:36-43).These are a few reasons He lets us go through it. I will cover more reasons later in this book.

If you will take the time and study the Scriptures for yourself, you will discover the deception that is believed by so many today. The first thing Jesus warned us about when He was asked about His second coming was for us not to be deceived (Matthew 24:4). Jesus comes back and raptures His chosen ones immediately after the tribulation (Matthew 24:29-31). And then pours out the "wrath of God" on the unbelievers all those that have aligned with the Antichrist and the False Prophet during the tribulation (Revelation 19:15). It is during the tribulation that those who take the "mark of the beast" that will suffer the "wrath of God." So we see from this the tribulation is not God's wrath, but Satan's wrath:

Therefore rejoice, O heavens, and you who dwell in them! Woe to the inhabitants of the earth and the sea! For the devil has come down to you, having great wrath, because he knows that he has a short time (Revelation 12:12).

We need to prepare spiritually, emotionally, and physically now to meet the Antichrist who is soon to appear. Those who think they will be raptured before the tribulation have little motivation to prepare, and many of them will be offended and fall away when persecution comes just like Jesus told us it would happen (Matthew 24:9-10).

We can make end-time prophecy simple by just sticking to what Scripture says. The Scriptures were written for the common folk to understand.

It is with great caution that I approach this subject not to add or take away from the Scriptures, because of a warning recorded in the book of Revelation:

"For I testify to everyone who hears the words of the prophecy of this book: If anyone adds to these things, God will add to him the plagues that are written in this book; and if anyone takes away from the words of the book of this prophecy, God shall take away his part from the Book of Life, from the holy city, and from the things which are written in this book" (Revelation 22:18-19).

Our attitude and how we go through the end-times is more important than most believe. Let me share a story that illustrates this truth:

During the Vietnam War Admiral James Stockdale's plane was shot down over North Vietnam. He was taken prisoner and beaten very severely. He spent the next seven and one half years in captivity, and four years of that time was in solitary confinement. He made it through his ordeal mainly because of his attitude.

In a book by James C. Collins titled *Good to Great*, Collins writes about a conversation he had with Admiral Stockdale regarding his coping strategy during his captivity in a Vietnamese Prisoner of War Camp.

When Collins asked him about how he made it through such a difficult time the Admiral answered:

"I never lost faith in the end of the story, I never doubted not only that I would get out, but also that I would prevail in the end, and turn the experience into the defining event of my life, which in retrospect, I would not trade."

When Collins was asked about the POWs that didn't make it out of Vietnam, Admiral Stockdale replied:

"Oh, that's easy, the optimists. Oh, they were the ones who said, 'We're going to be out by Christmas.' And Christmas would come, and Christmas would go. Then they'd say, 'We're going to be out by Easter.' And Easter would come, and Easter would go. And then 'Thanksgiving,' and then it would be Christmas again, and they lost hope and died of a broken heart."[1]

My prayer is you will keep an open mind and pray that God will show you the truth about the second coming of Christ.

---

[1] Collins, James C., 2010, *Good to Great*

INTRODUCTION

THE BOOK OF REVELATION IS THE REVELATION
of Jesus Christ. God gave us the book of Revelation to encourage us
and show that we will win in the end. He also gave it to us to help
us have faith when things start shaking around us.

Blessed is he who reads and those who hear the words of this
prophecy, and keep those things which are written in it; for the time
is near (Revelation 1:3).

We are told we are blessed if we read this book and hear what it
says and keep those things written in it.

In chapter one I begin with why we know there is a seven year
period of tribulation referred to as Daniel's Seventieth Week that
closes out this age. It is important to start here with this foundation,
because this is the backbone, so to speak, that helps us see where
the other prophesies fit.

In chapter two we will look at the signs Jesus gives us that precede His second coming. They are recorded in Matthew 24; Mark
13; Luke 21. I will be using Matthew chapter 24 where Jesus gives
a play by play announcement of the events that precede His second
coming in chronological order. Jesus really makes it simple for us to
understand, and He tells us exactly when the rapture will take place.

In chapter three I share how Paul the apostle tells us what has to
happen before we are raptured. He confirms what Jesus taught about
when the rapture takes place. He records this in II Thessalonians 2:1-4.

In chapter four I cover how John the apostle who received the book of Revelation reveals to us when the rapture takes place in Revelation chapter 20:4-6.

In chapter five I talk about the feasts of the Lord from Leviticus 23. Jesus fulfilled the Spring Feasts at His first coming and He will fulfill the Fall Feasts at His second coming. So the Fall Feasts are a rehearsal of the second coming and I will share what insights we can glean from them.

In chapter six I cover the signs that God is giving us from heaven. In Genesis chapter one God tells us the lights in the heavens are for signs and seasons.

In the gospel of Luke we read:

"And there will be signs in the sun, in the moon, and in the stars; and on the earth distress of nations, with perplexity, the sea and the waves roaring "(Luke 21:25).

"Now when these things begin to happen, look up and lift up your heads, because your redemption draws near" (Luke 21:28).

So when these signs begin to happen we are to look up because our redemption is near. In the last few years God has given us these signs, and I cover these signs and what they are conveying to us in this chapter.

Chapter seven is about the woman in Revelation twelve and the sign that appeared over Jerusalem September 23, 2017. It was exactly like the vision recorded by John the apostle in Revelation chapter 12 of the woman clothed with the sun, the moon at her feet, and twelve stars above her head. What does this mean?

In chapter eight I write about some of the assumptions that the Pre-Tribulation rapture doctrine is based on. We will look at the Greek to show how some Scriptures used to support this doctrine don't hold up under closer examination. Let me just give you one example:

*Because you have kept My command to persevere, I also will **keep** you from the hour of trial which shall come upon the whole world, to test those who dwell on the earth (Revelation 3:10).*

Let's look at what the word **keep** means in the Greek. The word is "Tereo" and it means; to attend to carefully; take care of; to guard; to keep one in the state in which he is.[2]

When we examine this Scripture more closely we realize it doesn't mention anything about a rapture, but that those that have kept His command to persevere will be protected.

It is the same Greek word "Tereo" Jesus used when He prayed that His followers would *not* be taken out the world, but that we would be kept from the evil one (John 17:15).

In chapter nine I talk about the falling away and I will share some things that can make your faith stronger and how you can stay faithful to the end. Satan is subtle and he doesn't want you to make it through what is coming. Therefore, it is important to know some things to avoid also.

One of the greatest reasons why Christians will fall away during the tribulation is they will be taking offense at what God is allowing. They don't understand that God is taking back this planet from Satan. Many will believe that God is punishing them and they will be offended. This is one of the reasons why it is so important to know the truth.

Chapter ten is about the millennial reign and a glimpse of what it might look like to give us HOPE for the future. Jesus endured the cross because of the joy that was set before Him. So as we focus on the joy that is set before us, it will help us get through the difficult times we are facing. In Isaiah we see many promises of the millennial reign that is coming to us. Jesus is going to comfort His people, give us beauty for ashes, joy for mourning, and the garment of praise for the spirit of heaviness (Isaiah 61:2-3).

Instead of your shame you shall have double honor, and instead of confusion they shall rejoice in their portion. Therefore in their land they shall possess double; everlasting joy shall be theirs (Isaiah 61:7).

---

[2] Strong, J., 1996, 5083, "Tereo" the Exhaustive Concordance

For those who have been plagued by condemnation and shame, He is going to give you double honor. We will have everlasting joy. Satan will be bound so the joy robber will be out of commission. Hallelujah!!!

Chapter eleven is about how to overcome fear. There are Biblical exercises we can use against this number one tool of the devil. Fear is rampant in our world today and we haven't seen the end of it. We need to be equipped to deal with fear in the coming days and I give some ways in this chapter that will help you combat this enemy.

I have included Scriptures on the seal judgments, trumpet judgments, and bowl judgments from Revelation in appendix A, B, and C.

CHAPTER ONE

DANIEL'S SEVENTIETH WEEK

I WILL BEGIN BY SHOWING WHERE WE GET Daniel's Seventieth Week from Scripture and how it is the last seven years just before Jesus returns. This is not the end of the world, but it is the end of this present age.

Most Christians agree that there is a seven year period of tribulation, but they differ on when the rapture happens in relationship to these seven years. For those who don't know what the rapture is, it is when Jesus returns and we are caught up to be with Him in the air. We will take a look at what the Bible says about the timing of the rapture in the next few chapters.

Daniel's Seventieth Week is divided into two periods of three and one half years and the last half is referred to as "Jacob's trouble" in Jeremiah:

Alas! For that day is great, So that none is like it; and it is the time of Jacob's trouble, but he shall be saved out of it 'For it shall come to pass in that day,' Says the Lord of hosts, 'That I will break his (Satan's) yoke from your neck, and will burst your bonds; foreigners shall no more enslave them (Jeremiah 30:7-8).

One thing that can help us face the days ahead is to understand we are being set-free when everything is shaking all around us.

Adam and Eve when they sinned they gave the ruler-ship of the earth over to Satan. God gets blamed for all the evil in the world today, but it was man's sin that allowed evil in and gave the kingdoms of the world to Satan; so he is the one responsible for all the wars, famines, hurricanes etc. Jesus took it back by living a sinless life and by dying on the cross, and He is coming back to take possession of it soon. Some wonder why God didn't just destroy the earth as soon as man sinned. The answer could be, where would we fit into this picture.

Maybe we need to renew our minds about the tribulation to see it as a positive thing and not a negative one. For one thing this time of trouble will force us out of our independent spirit into an interdependent spirit. It will bring unity amongst believers and we will increase our synergy levels of power. When that happens the Bible says we will be doing exploits (Daniel 11:32).

For then there will be great tribulation, such as has not been since the beginning of the world until this time, no, nor ever shall be (Matthew 24:21).

Jesus called this time the great tribulation and claims the rapture takes place immediately after it (Matthew 24:29-31).

We need to fasten our seat belts because of what is coming. It will be the worst time in human history and many people are oblivious to what they are about to experience, and many are ill prepared for it spiritually and physically.

Let's look at the prophecy in Daniel 9:24-27, and see what God will accomplish during this time.

Seventy weeks (seventy weeks of years or 490 years) are determined for your people and for your holy city, to finish the transgression, to make an end of sins, to make reconciliation for iniquity, to bring in everlasting righteousness, to seal up vision and prophecy, and to anoint the Most Holy (Daniel 9:24).

Know therefore and understand, that from the going forth of the command to restore and build Jerusalem until Messiah the Prince, there shall be seven weeks and sixty-two weeks; the street shall be built again, and the wall, even in troublesome times (Daniel 9:25).

And after the sixty-two weeks Messiah shall be cut off, but not for Himself; and the people of the prince who is to come shall destroy the city and the sanctuary. The end of it shall be with a flood, and till the end of the war desolations are determined (Daniel 9:26).

Then he (Antichrist) shall confirm a covenant with many for one week; but in the middle of the week he shall bring an end to sacrifice and offering and on the wing of abominations shall be one who makes desolate, even until the consummation, which is determined, is poured out on the desolate (Daniel 9:27).

When Jesus was crucified, and the prince that was to come which was the Roman General Titus who destroyed the city and sanctuary in 70 A.D, the first 69 weeks (483 years) of this prophecy were fulfilled leaving verse 27 to be fulfilled in the future by the Antichrist. Dates of Daniel 9:25-26 fulfillments are as follows:

"The weeks of years began with the commandment by Artaxerxes in 445 B.C. to restore Jerusalem. Chronologically, they are divided as: Seven sevens 49 years—445 to 396 B.C. (From Artaxerxes' decree to the arrival of Nehemiah and the covenant renewal celebration at Jerusalem) Sixty-two sevens 434 years—396 B.C. to A.D. 32 (From the dedication of the second temple to the crucifixion of the Lord Jesus Christ) One seven (7 years)—Unfulfilled."[3] There is a 2,000 year gap between Daniel 9:26 and 9:27.

Then he (Antichrist) shall confirm a covenant with many for one week; but in the middle of the week he shall bring an end to sacrifice and offering and on the wing of abominations shall be one who

[3] Nelson, Thomas, 1997, *Spirit Filled Life Study Bible*

makes desolate, even until the consummation, which is determined, is poured out on the desolate (Daniel 9:27).

Verse 27 is where we see there is a seven year tribulation that closes out this age. The "he" in verse 27 is the Antichrist, and he confirms a covenant with many for one week or a seven year period. Then, the Antichrist will break the covenant and attack Jerusalem three and one half years into the last seven years, and he will take over the temple and stop the sacrifices (Daniel 11:29-31). It is at this time he sits in the temple and claims to be God. This is when the great tribulation begins and lasts for three and one half years.

Many fall away from the faith under this pressure because their roots in the faith are not deep enough. The trials we are experiencing today are to get us ready for the time that is coming and causing our roots to go deeper. Those who take the "mark of the beast" during the last three and one half years will go on to experience the "wrath of God" which Jesus pours out after He returns (Isaiah 63:1-6; Revelation 19:11-16).

Some Scriptures that provide more information about the Antichrist and his objectives are:

He shall speak pompous words against the Most High, shall persecute the saints of the Most High, and shall intend to change times and law. Then the saints shall be given into his hand for a time and times and half a time (3½ years) (Daniel 7:25).

This is talking about the last three and one half years and the saints mentioned here at this time are the offspring of the woman (Revelation 12:13-17). The woman is being protected. This is answer to Jesus prayer (John 17:15).

And he (Antichrist) was given a mouth speaking great things and blasphemies, and he was given authority to continue for forty-two months (three and one half years). Then he opened his mouth in blasphemy against God, to blaspheme His name, His tabernacle, and those who dwell in heaven. It was granted to him to make war with the saints and to overcome them and authority was given him over every tribe, tongue, and nation. All who dwell on the earth will worship him, whose names have not been written in the Book of Life of the Lamb slain from the foundation of the world (Revelation 13:5-8).

The saints are persecuted but they ...*Overcome him by the blood of the lamb, the word of their testimony, and by not loving their lives to the end (Revelation 12:11).*

For whoever desires to save his life will lose it, but whoever loses his life for My sake and the gospel's will save it (Mark 8:35).

Another Scripture in Isaiah that refers to the Antichrist is:

Those who see you will gaze at you, and consider you, saying: "Is this the man who made the earth tremble, who shook kingdoms who made the world as a wilderness and destroyed its cities, Who did not open the house of his prisoners?" (Isaiah 14:16-17).

There is a warning in Scripture not to align with the Antichrist and the Babylonian system in the book of Revelation, or you will experience the vengeance of Almighty God (Revelation 18:4).

Note; a prophetic month is 30 days based on the lunar calendar and not the solar calendar. Therefore, in prophecy this adds up a 360 day year. Hence, we read about three and one half years recorded different ways in the word of God. It is referred 1260 days is some places, 42 months in other places, and time, times, and half a time in other places, but in all these cases it is talking about the last three and one half years.

CHAPTER TWO

THE RAPTURE
ACCORDING TO JESUS

MATTHEW CHAPTER 24 IS REFERRED TO AS the Olivet Discourse. There are two different prophecies in Matthew 24; one is a short range prophecy about the destruction of the temple, and one is long range prophecy about the second coming of Christ. The first prophecy is found in verses one and two.

Then Jesus went out and departed from the temple, and His disciples came up to show Him the buildings of the temple. And Jesus said to them, "Do you not see all these things? Assuredly, I say to you, not one stone shall be left here upon another, that shall not be thrown down" (Matthew 24:1-2).

This short range prophecy was fulfilled when Titus and his army destroyed the temple and burned it in 70 A.D. The gold melted and flowed down between the stones, and then the stones were torn down one by one to get the gold.

Now let's look at the long range prophecy of the second coming.

Now as He sat on the Mount of Olives, the disciples came to Him privately, saying, "Tell us, when will these things be? And what will be the sign of Your coming, and of the end of the age?"

And Jesus answered and said to them: "Take heed that no one deceives you. For many will come in My name, saying, 'I am the

Christ,' and will deceive many. And you will hear of wars and rumors of wars. See that you are not troubled; for all these things must come to pass, but the end is not yet. For nation will rise against nation, and kingdom against kingdom. And there will be famines, pestilences, and earthquakes in various places. All these are the beginning of sorrows" (Matthew 24:3-8).

In this passage Jesus begins laying out what to expect just before He returns. He says there will be deception, wars and rumors of wars, famines, pestilences, and earthquakes. Jesus referred to this time as the "beginning of sorrows," but He goes on to say, "But the end is not yet."

Then they will deliver you up to tribulation and kill you, and you will be hated by all nations for My name's sake. And then many will be offended, will betray one another, and will hate one another. Then many false prophets will rise up and deceive many. And because lawlessness will abound, the love of many will grow cold. But he who endures to the end shall be saved. And this gospel of the kingdom will be preached in all the world as a witness to all the nations, and then the end will come (Matthew 24:9-14).

In verses nine through fourteen, Jesus starts telling us about the persecution that is coming to Christians of all nations, and that many would be offended and fall away from the faith. This is because they were taught that they would not be here and now they are confused. They turn against other Christians and betray them and end up taking the "mark of the beast."

Many false prophets will arise doing signs and wonders, but Jesus said, *"You will know them by their fruits" (Matthew 7:15-16).*

And because of lawlessness abounding, the love of many will grow cold, but he who endures to the end will be saved. The great commission will be fulfilled at this time and then the end will come.

Jesus goes on to say:

Therefore when you see the "abomination of desolation", spoken of by Daniel the prophet, standing in the holy place (whoever reads, let him understand), then let those who are in Judea flee to the

8

mountains. Let him who is on the housetop not go down to take any-thing out of his house. And let him who is in the field not go back to get his clothes. But woe to those who are pregnant and to those who are nursing babies in those days! And pray that your flight may not be in winter or on the Sabbath. For then there will be great tribula-tion, such as has not been since the beginning of the world until this time, no, nor ever shall be. And unless those days were shortened, no flesh would be saved; but for the elect's sake those days will be shortened (Matthew 24:15-22).

When Jesus mentions the "abomination of desolation" in this passage, we know we are at the half way through Daniel's Seventieth Week, because we learned in the last chapter that the Antichrist sets up the "abomination of desolation" in the middle of the last seven years (Daniel 9:27).

He warns those who live in Judea to flee to the mountains, because this is when the Antichrist conquers Jerusalem. He causes the sacri-fices to cease and sits in the temple claiming to be God for the next three and one half years (Daniel 11:29-31; II Thessalonians 2:4}.

Now Jesus tells us when to expect the rapture.

Immediately after the tribulation of those days the sun will be darkened, and the moon will not give its light; the stars will fall from heaven, and the powers of the heavens will be shaken. Then the sign of the Son of Man will appear in heaven, and then all the tribes of the earth will mourn, and they will see the Son of Man coming on the clouds of heaven with power and great glory. And He will send His angels with a great sound of a trumpet, and they will gather together His elect from the four winds, from one end of heaven to the other (Matthew 24:29-31).

Jesus tells us the rapture takes place "immediately after the trib-ulation of those days." The key to keeping Bible prophecy simple is not by trying to figure it out with our logic, but it is just to believe what Scripture says. This is not complicated, but man in his logical thinking has made it confusing for many people.

When you see the Christians being persecuted in all nations, the great commission fulfilled, the new temple constructed and the "abomination of desolation" set up with the Antichrist sitting in the temple claiming to be God; then, know we are in the season for the rapture, but we have to see these prophesies fulfilled before there will be a rapture. We will see that Paul the apostle confirms this in the next chapter when he says the rapture happens after the "abomination of desolation" is set up.

CHAPTER THREE

THE RAPTURE ACCORDING TO PAUL THE APOSTLE

JESUS REVEALS TO US HE COMES BACK AND resurrects His elect after the great tribulation takes place. So let's see if Paul the apostle who wrote much of the New Testament confirms this. First He tells us about the resurrection and what to expect:

But I do not want you to be ignorant, brethren, concerning those who have fallen asleep, lest you sorrow as others who have no hope. For if we believe that Jesus died and rose again, even so God will bring with Him those who sleep in Jesus. For this we say to you by the word of the Lord, that we who are alive and remain until the coming of the Lord will by no means precede those who are asleep. For the Lord Himself will descend from heaven with a shout, with the voice of an archangel, and with the trumpet of God. And the dead in Christ will rise first. Then we who are alive and remain shall be caught up together with them in the clouds to meet the Lord in the air. And thus we shall always be with the Lord. Therefore comfort one another with these words (1 Thessalonians 4:13-18).

Paul wrote the Thessalonians about the resurrection to encourage them because they were being persecuted. A lie was circulating that the resurrection had already had taken place, so Paul wrote them a second letter telling them exactly when it would take place:

Now, brethren, concerning the coming of our Lord Jesus Christ and our gathering together to Him, we ask you, not to be soon shaken in mind or troubled, either by spirit or by word or by letter, as if from us, as though the day of Christ had come. Let no one deceive you by any means; for that Day will not come unless the falling away comes first, and the man of sin is revealed, the son of perdition, who opposes and exalts himself above all that is called God or that is worshiped, so that he sits as God in the temple of God, showing himself that he is God (II Thessalonians 2:1-4).

Paul says the rapture will *not* happen before there is a falling away and the Antichrist is sitting in the temple in Jerusalem claiming to be God." This confirms what Jesus taught about the rapture which eliminates it can happen now at any time.

Paul probably was taught this by those who were taught about it by Jesus, or by Jesus through the Holy Spirit, because they are in agreement the rapture will not take place before the tribulation.

The Jews need to build their third temple, and start their sacrifices before the Antichrist can come and take it over and stop the sacrifices and sit in the temple and claim to be God before there will be a rapture. This is simple and clear if we are going to believe the Scripture and what it says. You have to add to the word something that it is not saying to come up with a Pre-Trib rapture which goes against what Jesus and Paul are telling us.

At first glance we might come up with the conclusion that the rapture is in the middle of the seven years, but this is not what Paul is saying either. He is saying it cannot happen before then. The Mid-Trib rapture and the Pre-Wrath rapture doctrines even though they have the Church going through part the seven years still have the problem of explaining two second comings of Christ. This is why the Post-Trib rapture/ resurrection is the most Scripturally correct of all the different views.

Paul gives more revelation on the second coming when he says it happens at the "last trump." This means the rapture happens at the end of the great tribulation, because Jesus comes back at the "last trump."

Behold, I tell you a mystery: We shall not all sleep, but we shall all be changed— in a moment, in the twinkling of an eye, at the last trumpet. For the trumpet will sound, and the dead will be raised incorruptible, and we shall be changed. (1 Corinthians 15:51-52).

The context of chapter 15 of Corinthians is death will be dealt with which places the rapture after the great tribulation also. We know that death isn't completely overcome until after the one thousand year reign of Christ is over and we go into eternity, but people will live much longer lives again like in the beginning (Isaiah 65:20).

To say the people of God are *not* going to be here during Daniel's Seventieth Week is actually to miss the purpose of why God is allowing us to be here.

Those who do wickedly against the covenant he (Antichrist) shall corrupt with flattery; but the people who know their God shall be strong, and carry out great exploits. And those of the people who understand shall instruct many; yet for many days they shall fall by sword and flame, by captivity and plundering. Now when they fall, they shall be aided with a little help; but many shall join with them by intrigue. And some of those of understanding shall fall, to refine them, purify them, and make them white, until the time of the end; because it is still for the appointed time (Daniel 11:32-35).

This Scripture in Daniel says the ones who know their God will be strong and carry out great exploits. They will be warning those who will listen, not to take the "mark of the beast." They will lead many to Christ and we know there is great revival that happens during the great tribulation (Revelation 7:9). This is harvest time. The bride of Christ will also be made ready for her Husband during the tribulation. The tribulation will bring unity amongst believers. The Church is divided today into different denominations and that will cease when persecution comes and believers have to go underground.

Paul adds a few more reasons why the saints are here during the tribulation in Second Thessalonians:

We are bound to thank God always for you, brethren, as it is fitting, because your faith grows exceedingly, and the love of every one of you all abounds toward each other, so that we ourselves boast of you among the Churches of God for your patience and faith in all your persecutions and tribulations that you endure, which is manifest evidence of the righteous judgment of God, that you may be counted worthy of the kingdom of God, for which you also suffer; since it is a righteous thing with God to repay with tribulation those who trouble you, and to give you who are troubled rest with us when the Lord Jesus is revealed from heaven with His mighty angels, in flaming fire taking vengeance on those who do not know God, and on those who do not obey the gospel of our Lord Jesus Christ. These shall be punished with everlasting destruction from the presence of the Lord and from the glory of His power, when He comes, in that Day, to be glorified in His saints and to be admired among all those who believe, because our testimony among you was believed (II Thessalonians 1:3-10).

We are being allowed to go through tribulation to increase our faith and to confirm we are accounted worthy for the kingdom. Also, a righteous God cannot bring vengeance on the wicked if they have done nothing wrong. So these are some more reasons why God allows us to go through the great tribulation. God doesn't test anyone, but He allows his people to be tested to prove that we are faithful and for us to realize how much we love God and that He lives in us, because it takes God to love God.

So we can see that even though the tribulation is Satan's wrath, God will use it for good for those who love him and are called according to His purpose (Romans 8:28).

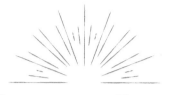

CHAPTER FOUR

THE RAPTURE ACCORDING TO JOHN THE APOSTLE

LET'S LOOK NOW AT WHEN JOHN THE APOSTLE says the rapture takes place.

And I saw thrones, and they sat on them, and judgment was committed to them. Then I saw the souls of those who had been beheaded for their witness to Jesus and for the word of God, who had not worshiped the beast or his image, and had not received his mark on their foreheads or on their hands. And they lived and reigned with Christ for a thousand years, but the rest of the dead did not live again until the thousand years were finished. This is the first resurrection. Blessed and holy is he who has part in the first resurrection. Over such the second death has no power, but they shall be priests of God and of Christ, and shall reign with Him a thousand years (Revelation 20:4-6).

The first resurrection mentioned in this Scripture is the rapture of the church and it includes the martyrs who would *not* take the "mark of the beast" which is given out the last three and one half years of Daniel's Seventieth Week. This rapture includes all those who are believers in Jesus that are dead or alive, but this passage is focused on these martyrs. So we see John says the rapture is after the tribulation too.

15

One of the reasons it is important to know the truth of when the resurrection takes place is because if we think we are going to escape persecution, and don't understand why it is happening we will be disillusioned and be tempted to think God has abandoned us, and that makes us a candidate to fall away from the faith, so some of us are writing about it in the hope to help some see through the deception that is rampart among believers.

We do not have to fear what is coming if we are "In Christ." This is someone who has received Christ and been baptized in the Holy Spirit.

We are to repent from our sins and come to Him and ask His forgiveness; and to get the Holy Spirit you need to ask for it to receive it (Luke 11:9-13).

This makes Christianity different from other religions, because all other religions are based on you earning heaven by your works, and then they fail to get you there in the end, because Jesus Christ is the only name under heaven whereby you can be saved. He is God in the flesh and if you want God He is the only one that can save you.

Peter said:

Nor is there salvation in any other, for there is no other name under heaven given among men by which we must be saved (Acts 4:12).

Jesus said to him, *"I am the way, the truth, and the life. No one comes to the Father except through Me" (John 14:6).*

I am praying that this book will find its way into the hands of those that are seeking the truth, and it helps them to grow in their faith and helps them endure to the end.

CHAPTER FIVE

THE FEASTS OF THE LORD

THE SEVEN FEASTS OF THE LORD ARE PRO-phetic. We know this because the Spring Feasts were fulfilled by Jesus right down to the day and hour of His First Coming. The Fall Feasts are rehearsal of the second coming of Christ. The summer between the Spring Feasts and the Fall Feasts is representative of the last 2,000 years.

Spring Feasts: Fulfilled at the first coming of Jesus:

Feast of Passover or Pesach	Nissan 14 Leviticus 23: 4-5	Fulfilled by Christ, Lamb of God on the Cross
Feast of Unleavened Bread	Nissan 15 Leviticus 23:6-8	Fulfilled by Christ living a sinless life
Feast of First Fruits	First day after the Sabbath Leviticus 23:9-14	Fulfilled by Christ at His resurrection

1 7

Shavuot the Festival of Weeks or Pentecost	Fifty days after Feast of First Fruits Leviticus 23:15-22	Fulfilled on the Day of Pentecost

Fall Feasts: Six months after Spring Feasts to be fulfilled at the second coming:

Feast of Trumpets (Rosh Hashanah)	Tishrei 1 Leviticus 23:23-25	Jesus returns at the "Last Trump"
Day of Atonement (Yom-Kippur)	Tishrei 10 Leviticus 23:26-32	Armageddon
Feast of Tabernacles (Sukkot)	Tishrei 15 Leviticus 23:33-35	Marriage Supper of the Lamb

Jesus gave us a clue that He was coming back on the Feast of Trumpets when He said, *"But of that day and hour no one knows, not even the angels of heaven, but My Father only" (Matthew 24:36).*

The Feast of Trumpets is the only feast that no one knows the day or hour it begins. This is because it is the only feast that begins a month. Two witnesses of the Sanhedrin have to witness the sliver of the new moon and blow their trumpets to begin this feast; hence, nobody knows the day or hour.

The Fall Feasts start with the Feast of Trumpets on Tishrei 1. Ten days later, the Day of Atonement begins on Tishrei 10. Five days later, the Feast of Tabernacles begins on Tishrei 15 and continues for the next eight days.

One of the insights that the Fall Feasts gives us is that the second coming is not a one day event, but takes place over several days. I see Jesus coming back on the Feast of Trumpets to rapture His chosen ones, and then He leads a military campaign up through Jordan for the next ten days as the kings of the east surround Jerusalem ending with Armageddon on the Day of Atonement (Psalm 2; Isaiah 63:1-6; Habakkuk 3). Then, five days later the Feast to Tabernacles begins with the "marriage supper of the Lamb" taking place at that time.

When we hear the seventh trumpet we will see our Lord coming with the clouds and every eye will see Him:

Behold, He is coming with clouds, and every eye will see Him, even they who pierced Him. And all the tribes of the earth will mourn because of Him. Even so, Amen (Revelation 1:7).

Traditionally, watchfulness was a critical ingredient of the Feast of Trumpets. This need for watchfulness and preparedness in connection with the Feast of Trumpets is echoed and re-echoed throughout the New Testament in connection with the Lord's second coming:

Watch therefore; for you know not what hour your Lord comes (Matthew 24:42).

Therefore, let us not sleep, as do others, but let us watch and be sober-minded (I Thessalonians 5:6).

If Jesus comes back on the Fall Feasts this would mean Daniel's Seventieth Week should begin on the Fall Feasts seven years earlier when the Antichrist confirms a covenant with many (Daniel 9:27). Then we would see the "abomination of desolation" set up three and one half years later when the Antichrist conquers Jerusalem.

When we see a covenant confirmed by the Antichrist we will know there are seven years before Jesus returns; and when the "abomination of desolation" is set up with the Antichrist sitting in the temple claiming to be God; we will know there is three and one half years before the Lord returns. This is another advantage of knowing Bible prophecy.

CHAPTER SIX

SIGNS IN THE HEAVENS

In Genesis we read:

THEN GOD SAID, "LET THERE BE LIGHTS IN THE *firmament of the heavens to divide the day from the night; and let them be for signs and seasons, and for days and years" (Genesis 1:14).*

God says let there be lights in the heavens for signs and seasons.

A lunar eclipse produces a red moon that resembles blood. A blood moon is said to be an omen for Israel, while a solar eclipse is said to be an omen for the world.

There were two blood moons in 2014, and two in 2015 that took place on God's feast days. This is a very rare occurrence and has only happened four times in the last 500 years. Each time they appeared in this sequence there were major events that took place with the Jews.

When these signs appeared on God's feast days in 1492-93, Spain persecuted the Jews and banished them from their country if they would not convert to Catholicism.

The next time they appeared was in 1949-50, right after the Jews returned to their homeland; six Arab nations planned to attack Israel, and with America's help Israel won this battle. American pilots repaired some World War II planes, and destroyed Egypt's Air Force with a surprised attack before Egypt had a chance to attack Israel.

Then the blood moons occurred again in 1966-67, when Israel won the six day war after being attacked. Israel took possession of Jerusalem as a result.

These signs appeared again in 2014 and 2015, one on Passover and one on the Feast of Tabernacles of each year. Israel-Gaza conflict, also known as Protective Edge was a military operation launched by Israel on July 8, 2014 in Hamas-ruled Gaza strip after Hamas captured three Israeli teenagers and murdered them. Israel responded and Hamas started firing rockets into Israel, and a seven week conflict broke out. Israel destroyed many tunnels that were being dug to cross into Israel. This war resulted in the death of thousands Palestinians and this took place right after the blood moon on Passover 2014. These blood moons could mean some bigger stuff in on the way also...

On August 21, 2017 a solar eclipse came across America and the moment it left the United States and entered the Atlantic Ocean hurricane Harvey started brewing and four days later on August 25 it hit Southern Texas causing a lot of damage. Notice that this solar eclipse and the hurricane Harvey happened on the same dates of the Scripture reference of Luke 21:25; August 21st and 25th). Do you think that is a coincidence or God's signature?

And there will be signs in the sun, in the moon, and in the stars; and on the earth distress of nations, with perplexity, the sea and the waves roaring; men's hearts failing them from fear and the expectation of those things which are coming on the earth, for the powers of the heavens will be shaken. Then they will see the Son of Man coming in a cloud with power and great glory. Now when these things begin to happen, look up and lift up your heads, because your redemption draws near (Luke 21:25-28).

Luke 21:25 says there will be signs in the sun and sea waves roaring; and in verse 28 it says when you see these signs start looking up, because your redemption is near. This Scripture isn't the second coming, but telling us it is near.

Some people have pointed out there is another solar eclipse coming across America April 8, 2024, and when you plot their courses they form an X right over the New Madrid Fault right in the center of America. Is this a warning of a major earthquake that is coming and when?

Add to these signs another sign in the Zodiac that took place in the heavens September 23, 2017, which is actually a great sign. It is the formation of the woman Virgo clothed with the sun, the moon under her feet, and with twelve stars over her head. This is an exact picture of what John the apostle saw and records in Revelation chapter twelve.

It appears God is revealing to us that the time of the second coming of Christ is near, even at the door, but we know that it will be preceded by Daniel's Seventieth Week.

This means if you are a born-again Christian your redemption draws near, but it also means that the tribulation time just before the second coming is near, and we should be preparing for it.

This time that is coming we need to prepare for spiritually, emotionally, and physically.

Some of the ways to prepare are:
1. Make sure you are filled with the Holy Spirit (Luke 11:11-13; Acts 2:38-39).
2. Working on your relationship with the Lord by reading His word, talking to Him in prayer with some added fasting, praising Him, worshipping Him (Joel 2:12; John 4:23).
3. By cultivating a thankful heart (1 Thessalonians 5:18).
4. By laying aside every weight and repenting of any sin (Psalm 139:23-24; Hebrews 12:1).
5. By staying in fellowship with other Christians (Hebrews 10:25).
6. By counting it all joy when in tribulation (Romans 5:1-5; James 1:2).

7. By using our gifts of the Holy Spirit to help build up the body of Christ and ourselves too.
8. By storing up some food and water (Proverbs 30:25).

Therefore, brethren, having boldness to enter the Holiest by the blood of Jesus, by a new and living way which He consecrated for us, through the veil, that is, His flesh, and having a High Priest over the house of God, let us draw near with a true heart in full assurance of faith, having our hearts sprinkled from an evil conscience and our bodies washed with pure water. Let us hold fast the confession of our hope without wavering, for He who promised is faithful. And let us consider one another in order to stir up love and good works, not forsaking the assembling of ourselves together, as is the manner of some, but exhorting (encouraging) one another, and so much the more as you see the Day approaching (Hebrews 10:19-25).

I believe those who prepare using these disciplines not in a legalistic way, but as the Lord leads will go to a new level of power in God and do greater works that Jesus said we would do, because He was going to the Father (John 14:12). Jesus commissioned His followers to heal the sick, raise the dead, and cast out demons (Matthew 10:8). It is up to us to do the healing now. He has given us the authority to do so. Every time I have been healed is when another brother or sister commanded it to be done.

If you have the Holy Spirit you have the same Holy Spirit Jesus had to do miracles. Of course, He only did what the Father showed Him to do. So we have the authority and as we are led by the Holy Spirit we can do these miracles. Jesus is still healing people today through His servants; so step out in faith and God will meet you there, and you will be amazed at what God can accomplish through you.

A healing revival is coming to the Church in these last days and is already here, and it is possible that you could be one of the ones God uses to heal others and do some of exploits that the book of Daniel says we will be doing.

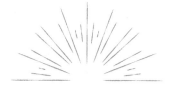

CHAPTER SEVEN

THE WOMAN IN
REVELATION TWELVE

NOW A GREAT SIGN APPEARED IN HEAVEN: A *woman clothed with the sun, with the moon under her feet, and on her head a garland of twelve stars. Then being with child, she cried out in labor and in pain to give birth. And another sign appeared in heaven: behold, a great, fiery red dragon having seven heads and ten horns, and seven diadems on his heads. His tail drew a third of the stars of heaven and threw them to the earth. And the dragon stood before the woman who was ready to give birth, to devour her child as soon as it was born. She bore a male child who was to rule all nations with a rod of iron. And her Child was caught up to God and His throne. Then the woman fled into the wilderness, where she has a place prepared by God that they should feed her there one thousand two hundred and sixty days (Revelation 12:1-6).*

This is a symbolic picture that shows the drama of the war between good and evil that closes out the age. We have a woman that represents Israel. She gives birth to a male child Jesus who will rule over the nations with a rod of iron.

We have a red dragon who is Satan and he tries to kill the child, but the child is caught up to God and His throne.

Then the dragon goes after the woman and she flees into the wilderness where God has a place prepared for her for 1260 days or the last three and one half years of this age.

So this prophecy jumps ahead 2,000 years to the time of the end. This prophecy has a double fulfillment once with the birth of Jesus and second fulfillment of those who will rule and reign with Jesus which this sign appearing on September 23, 2017 revealed to us:

And I saw thrones, and they sat on them, and judgment was committed to them. Then I saw the souls of those who had been beheaded for their witness to Jesus and for the word of God, who had not worshiped the beast or his image, and had not received his mark on their foreheads or on their hands. And they lived and reigned with Christ for a thousand years. But the rest of the dead did not live again until the thousand years were finished. This is the first resurrection. Blessed and holy is he who has part in the first resurrection. Over such the second death has no power, but they shall be priests of God and of Christ, and shall reign with Him a thousand years (Revelation 20:4-6).

These martyrs will rule and reign with Jesus during His millennial reign.

The woman in chapter twelve 2,000 years ago was Israel, but today it is Israel and the Gentiles combined. All those who believe in Jesus are of the seed of Abraham. This is because the Gentiles have been grafted into the olive tree (Israel) (Romans 11:17). This isn't replacement theology, but it is inclusive theology. Jesus came to save the Gentiles too.

For you are all sons of God through faith in Christ Jesus. For as many of you as were baptized into Christ have put on Christ. There is neither Jew nor Greek, there is neither slave nor free, there is neither male nor female; for you are all one in Christ Jesus. And if you are Christ's, then you are Abraham's seed, and heirs according to the promise (Galatians 3:26-29).

Chapter twelve reads on:

And war broke out in heaven: Michael and his angels fought with the dragon; and the dragon and his angels fought, but they did not prevail, nor was a place found for them in heaven any longer. So the great dragon was cast out, that serpent of old, called the Devil and Satan, who deceives the whole world; he was cast to the earth, and his angels were cast out with him. Then I heard a loud voice saying in heaven, "Now salvation, and strength, and the kingdom of our God, and the power of His Christ have come, for the accuser of our brethren, who accused them before our God day and night, has been cast down. And they overcame him by the blood of the Lamb and by the word of their testimony, and they did not love their lives to the death. Therefore rejoice O heavens, and you who dwell in them! Woe to the inhabitants of the earth and the sea! For the devil has come down to you, having great wrath, because he knows that he has a short time" (Revelation 12:7-12).

Satan is cast out of heaven to possess the Antichrist these last three and one half years. This is the trinity of evil Satan, the Antichrist, and the False Prophet. We can see why Jesus said this would be the worst time in history because we see the devil is on the loose.

We see the brethren, the Church, is still here at this time. It appears now salvation is announced and has come because the accuser of the brethren has been cast down. The good news is these brethren win and defeat the Antichrist by the blood of the Lamb, the word of the testimony and by not loving their lives, but by laying them down for a cause. If what you are living for is not worth dying for, then consider living for something that is worth dying for. These martyrs that were beheaded because they would not submit to the Antichrist will rise again with a resurrected body to never die again and live to rule and reign with Jesus. Those believers that are not destined for martyrdom are protected for these last three and one half years.

Now when the dragon saw that he had been cast to the earth, he persecuted the woman who gave birth to the male Child. But the woman was given two wings of a great eagle, that she might fly into the wilderness to her place, where she is nourished for a time and times and half a time, from the presence of the serpent. So the serpent spewed water out of his mouth like a flood after the woman that he might cause her to be carried away by the flood. But the earth helped the woman, and the earth opened its mouth and swallowed up the flood which the dragon had spewed out of his mouth. And the dragon was enraged with the woman, and he went to make war with the rest of her offspring, who keep the commandments of God and have the testimony of Jesus Christ (Revelation 12:13-17).

We can see this demonic spirit in the world today persecuting Christians and trying to destroy Israel. But this Scripture is referring to the last three and one half years when it will intensify, because the devil knows his time is short.

We are going to defeat the enemy with weapons that are spiritual, so today it the time to start using them.

For the weapons of our warfare are not carnal but mighty in God for pulling down strongholds, casting down arguments and every high thing that exalts itself against the knowledge of God, bringing every thought into captivity to the obedience of Christ (II Corinthians 10:4-5).

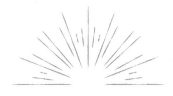

Cʜᴀᴘᴛᴇʀ Eɪɢʜᴛ

Sᴇᴠᴇɴ Pʀᴇ-Tʀɪʙᴜʟᴀᴛɪᴏɴ Rᴀᴘᴛᴜʀᴇ Aꜱꜱᴜᴍᴘᴛɪᴏɴꜱ

Aɴ ᴀꜱꜱᴜᴍᴘᴛɪᴏɴ ᴏʀ ɪɴꜰᴇʀᴇɴᴄᴇ ɪꜱ ᴀ ʟᴏɢɪᴄᴀʟ conclusion from something Scripture does say to something it does not say. It is believed to be compatible and consistent with Scripture whereas it is not.

Let's look at some of inferences that the Pre-Trib doctrine is based on. I mentioned this first one in the introduction, but I would like talk about it again, because it is a perfect example of what I mean by something sounding true when it is not.

1.   The inference: We are raptured before the tribulation because of what we read in Revelation 3:10:

Because you have kept My command to persevere, I also will **keep** *you from the hour of trial which shall come upon the whole world, to test those who dwell on the earth (Revelation 3:10).*

Let's look at the word **keep** in the Greek:

5083 τηρέω [tereo /tay·reh·o/] v. 1 to attend to carefully, take care of. 1a to guard. 1b metaph. to keep, one in the state in which he is. 1c to observe. 1d to reserve: to undergo something.[4]

---

[4]   Strong, J., 1996, *The Exhaustive Concordance of the Bible*

When we take a closer look at this verse we see it does not say anything about being raptured, but the contrary. It is the same Greek word used by Jesus in John 17:15

I do not pray that You should take them out of the world, but that You should keep (tereo) them from the evil one (John 17:15).

This is great example of how one can make Scripture say something it doesn't really say. It may sound good, but it is a lie.

2. The inference: The tribulation is God's wrath, so the Church is raptured before the tribulation:

For God did not appoint us to wrath, but to obtain salvation through our Lord Jesus Christ (I Thessalonians. 5:9).

Why this inference is inaccurate:

This Scripture says believers are *not* appointed to wrath. It doesn't say they are raptured. It is assumed that the tribulation is the "wrath of God" when it is not. I have already covered that in a previous chapter, so I won't say any more about that here.

3. The inference: John taken to heaven which is a type and shadow of the rapture of the Church before the tribulation:

After these things I looked, and behold, a door standing open in heaven. And the first voice which I heard was like a trumpet speaking with me, saying, "Come up here, and I will show you things which must take place after this"(Revelation 4:1).

Why this inference is inaccurate:

This verse does not say the Church is taken to heaven, it says John was, but it is inferred to say that the Church is raptured before Daniel's Seventieth Week.

This is adding to Scripture something it does not say and we are warned not to do that (Revelation 22:18).

4. The inference: Christians are raptured before Daniel's Seventieth Week, because it is referred to as Jacob's trouble in Jeremiah:

Why this inference is inaccurate:

It is assumed that because Daniel's Seventieth Week is referred to as Jacob's trouble it is only for the Jews, so this means the Church is raptured before the tribulation. The Bible doesn't say anything about the believers in Jesus being raptured before it takes place. This is an assumption that is not based on any solid evidence, but it is another example of man's logic getting involved. Also, I will point out that Jacob now includes the Gentile believers (the Church) which I have explained already.

5. The inference: Two separate returns because there is Scripture that says Jesus is coming for His saints and with His saints:

For this we say to you by the word of the Lord, that we who are alive and remain until the coming of the Lord will by no means precede those who are asleep. For the Lord Himself will descend from heaven with a shout, with the voice of an archangel, and with the trumpet of God. And the dead in Christ will rise first. Then we who are alive and remain shall be caught up together with them in the clouds to meet the Lord in the air. And thus we shall always be with the Lord. Therefore comfort one another with these words (I Thessalonians 4:13-18).

FOR is the key word. Jesus is coming *for* His saints

Now Enoch, the seventh from Adam, prophesied about the second coming also saying:

Behold, the Lord comes with ten thousands of His saints, to execute judgment on all, to convict all who are ungodly among them of all their ungodly deeds which they have committed in an ungodly way, and of all the harsh things which ungodly sinners have spoken against Him (Jude 14-15).

WITH is the key word. Jesus is coming *with* His saints:

Why this inference is inaccurate:

These are different verses using different words to describe the same event. Scholars have taken this coming *for* and *with* and made the assumption that there are two separate comings of the Lord instead of seeing this is two different perspectives of the same event.

Jesus comes through the clouds *FOR* His saints and they are caught up in the air to be with Him, and then He continues to travel to the earth *WITH* His saints to execute judgment on the wicked.

6. The Inference: The Church is raptured because it is not mentioned after chapter four in Revelation:

Why this inference is inaccurate:

The church is referred to many times *after* chapter four of Revelation only by different names. It is referred symbolically as a woman. We see the Church referred to as brethren in chapter twelve of Revelation, and as saints in chapters thirteen and fourteen. It is referred as the bride of Christ at the second coming of Jesus (Revelation 19:7). So this is an oversight that the Church is not here during the tribulation.

This is another attempt to defend a doctrine that has deceived so many in the body of Christ today and is giving them a false hope. Those that believe that they are not going to be here are *not* preparing for what they are about to experience and that is why God is trying to wake them up.

7. The inference: His return could happen at any time:

Why this inference is inaccurate:

But you, brethren, are not in darkness, so that this Day should overtake you as a thief. You are all sons of light and sons of the day. We are not of the night nor of darkness. Therefore let us not sleep, as others do, but let us watch and be sober. For those who sleep, sleep at night, and those who get drunk are drunk at night. But let us who are of the day be sober, putting on the breastplate of faith and love, and as a helmet the hope of salvation (I Thessalonians 5:4-8).

It will come on unbelievers like a thief, but not the believers that know their Bible. Jesus and the apostles John and Paul have told us of events that have to happen before the rapture. So this eliminates it can happen at any time. We will be here to see the destruction that comes on the wicked just like Psalm 91 declares:

A thousand may fall at your side, and ten thousand at your right hand; but it shall not come near you. Only with your eyes shall you look, and see the reward of the wicked (Psalm 91:7-8).

The arguments for the Pre-Trib rapture doctrine are persuasive because they are based on logic. Satan has used man's logic to seduce believers into a belief that is a lie so he can get them confused and doubting God's love for them when they find themselves in the middle of the tribulation. We are going to have to know the truth to make it through what is coming soon.

CHAPTER NINE

THE GREAT FALLING AWAY

JESUS TELLS US THAT MANY WILL FALL AWAY from the faith and because of lawlessness the love of many will grow cold. He says Christians will betray one another. The main reason for this falling away is a lack of understanding of what God is doing and many becoming offended.

Many believe things are going to continue on as they have in the past and they don't realize that we are in a period of rapid change. Many are ill prepared spiritually and physically. My reason for writing this book is help them see what is coming and help them prepare to meet it successfully.

We know the falling away will take place during the great tribulation because both Jesus and Paul referred to it in the context of the "abomination of desolation." It is the persecution of the saints by the Antichrist that triggers it.

In the parable of the sower Jesus mentions the seed sown in rocky soil that their roots didn't go deep, and when persecution comes they stumble. The Greek word for stumble can also be translated offence.

It appears John the Baptist even fell into offense when Jesus wasn't doing what He expected the Messiah to do. He sent his disciples to Jesus to ask him if he was the Messiah. If anyone should have known that Jesus was the Messiah it should have been John. This shows how intense the battle will be in the end-times and how hard it will be to hang on to our faith. We will need to be filled with the Holy Spirit to endure. Jesus sent word back to John and say:

"And blessed is he who is not offended because of Me" *(Matthew 11:6).*

We don't have to take offense and fall away if we are in fellowship with other believers and prayed up. We need to understand what and why God is doing the things He is doing. This is why He gave us 150 chapters in the Bible that relate to the end-times.

It will help us to prepare today by confessing and forsaking our sins, which will deepen our relationship with other Christians and the Lord. We will need an intimate relationship with the Lord to be able to stand against the Antichrist and not fall away from the faith. This is a time to be a Mary and sit at His feet and get to know our Lord.

We must remember Jesus is the one who is opening the seals of Revelation. Nothing you are experiencing or will experience surprises Him. If you are blaming God for what is happening during the end-times you will be offended by Him, so cultivating a thankful heart now will go a long way.

To continue with the parable of the sower; the thorny ground represents those who have been deceived by the cares of this life and deceitfulness of riches. They think more money is the answer to their problems. We cannot serve mammon (money) and God at the same time, because we cannot serve two masters (Matthew 6:24). We must decide which one will be our God. It is not a sin to work for money, but we need to put our faith in Jesus and not the dollar bill:

But seek first the kingdom of God and His righteousness, and all these things shall be added to you. Therefore do not worry about tomorrow, for tomorrow will worry about its own things. Sufficient for the day is its own trouble (Matthew 6:33-34).

If we fix our eyes upon Jesus and press into knowing Him in a deeper way the things of this world will lose their grip on us. Then we will be able to walk in the Spirit and receive the fruit of the Spirit into our life:

And do this, knowing the time, that now it is high time to awake out of sleep; for now our salvation is nearer than when we first believed. The night is far spent, the day is at hand. Therefore let us cast off the works of darkness, and let us put on the armor of light. Let us walk properly, as in the day, not in revelry and drunkenness, not in lewdness and lust, not in strife and envy. But put on the Lord Jesus Christ, and make no provision for the flesh, to fulfill its lusts (Romans 13:11-14).

But I discipline my body and bring it into subjection, lest, when I have preached to others, I myself should become disqualified (I Corinthians 9:27).

A three day fast will break most strongholds if we have any strongholds and most of us do if we will be honest. Fasting humbles our flesh and puts it under subjection to our spirit, so maybe that is why fasting is a hard thing for most of us.

University of Southern California has done research that claims a three day fast rejuvenates our immune system. One day a week could be a start for those who have difficulty fasting.

We have looked at some behaviors that will cause people to fall away or become unfruitful. Some of them are fear of persecution, picking up an offense, the cares of this life, and deceitfulness of riches (greed), alcohol, lust, and strife. We can add abuse, gluttony, and basically any area we have not surrendered to the Lord. Instead of medicating our pain with some vice, we should pray that our pain would compel us to press into Jesus.

We have looked at some behaviors that will strengthen our faith too. Some of them are working on our relationship with the Lord, repenting of our sins, staying in fellowship and adding some fasting to our prayers.

I believe it will take a prayer and fasting lifestyle to get through these times that are coming. We should pray and ask God what He would have us do. The good news if you are a follower of Jesus He promises us that His grace is sufficient to help us meet whatever we have to go through, and He is the author and finisher of our faith (Hebrews 12:1-2).

I close this chapter with a few Scriptures that can help in times of persecution:

Blessed are those who are persecuted for righteousness' sake, for theirs is the kingdom of heaven. Blessed are you when they revile and persecute you, and say all kinds of evil against you falsely for My sake. Rejoice and be exceedingly glad, for great is your reward in heaven, for so they persecuted the prophets who were before you (Matthew 5:10-12).

We shouldn't take persecution personally, because it is Jesus in us that this world hates. Christians are dead and buried in baptism with Christ and then raised to newness of life with Jesus living in them. So it is Jesus that Satan hates and this is the reason we are persecuted. The first century Christians realized this and they rejoiced by being accounted worthy to suffer for the Lord.

None of us like to suffer, but if we understand why, it helps; it is a momentary light affliction that is creating an eternal weight of glory for us. When we are persecuted:

Jesus says, *"Rejoice and be exceedingly glad, for great is your reward in heaven."*

I know a sister in the Lord during the Jesus revival of the sixties and seventies who became concerned when she wasn't going through a trial, because she knew it is trials that help us grow in our relationship with God.

Bless those who persecute you; bless and do not curse. Rejoice with those who rejoice, and weep with those who weep. Be of the same mind toward one another. Do not set your mind on high things, but associate with the humble. Do not be wise in your own opinion. Repay no one evil for evil. Have regard for good things in the sight of all men. If it is possible, as much as depends on you, live peaceably with all men. Beloved, do not avenge yourselves, but rather give place to wrath; for it is written, "Vengeance is Mine, I will repay," says the Lord (Romans 12:13-19).

These disciplines we are encouraged to do are not possible in our own strength and this is why we need to seek to be filled with the Holy Spirit daily, and in a busy world like ours this will take discipline on our part to spend time at the feet of Jesus to get our daily bread before we run off into the busy world. This means we are going have to sacrifice some things that are robbing us of this time of fellowship with our Lord.

I have asked the Lord about protecting myself from the enemy and using methods of self-defense like firearms. What I hear from Him is, "He who lives by the sword dies by the sword." So I think this is a personal matter between you and the Lord.

But we have this treasure in earthen vessels that the excellence of the power may be of God and not of us. We are hard-pressed on every side, yet not crushed; we are perplexed, but not in despair; persecuted, but not forsaken; struck down, but not destroyed— always carrying about in the body the dying of the Lord Jesus, that the life of Jesus also may be manifested in our body. For we who live are always delivered to death for Jesus' sake, that the life of Jesus also may be manifested in our mortal flesh. So then death is working in us, but life in you.

And since we have the same spirit of faith, according to what is written, "I believed and therefore I spoke," we also believe and therefore speak, knowing that He who raised up the Lord Jesus will also raise us up with Jesus, and will present us with you. For all things are for your sakes, that grace, having spread through the many, may cause thanksgiving to abound to the glory of God.

Therefore we do not lose heart. Even though our outward man is perishing, yet the inward man is being renewed day by day. For our light affliction, which is but for a moment, is working for us a far more exceeding and eternal weight of glory, while we do not look at the things which are seen, but at the things which are not seen. For the things which are seen are temporary, but the things which are not seen are eternal (II Corinthians 4:7-18).

It is in the times of persecution when we need to remember that there is a resurrection coming for those who remain faithful to the end.

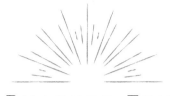

CHAPTER TEN

THE MILLENNIAL
REIGN OF CHRIST

This chapter will give you HOPE for the future.

OUR IMAGINATIONS CAN BE USED FOR GOOD

or evil. If our imaginations are aligned with the word of God, they can be useful and good.

Therefore we also, since we are surrounded by so great a cloud of witnesses, let us lay aside every weight, and the sin which so easily ensnares us, and let us run with endurance the race that is set before us, looking unto Jesus, the author and finisher of our faith, who for the joy that was set before Him endured the cross, despising the shame, and has sat down at the right hand of the throne of God (Hebrews 12:1-2).

There is some important information in this Scripture on how we can endure what it coming. Notice that one of things that helped Jesus to endure the cross was the "joy that was set before Him." Looking at the joy that is set before us as believers in Christ can help us get through some hard times that are coming.

What are some of the things that Jesus might have imagined that brought Him joy? Could it be that He was going to save God's creation and give it back to the Father after He restored us and the earth? We don't know for sure, because we can only imagine.

So what are some of the promises in the word of God that we can imagine that will give us joy? What about the multitude that will come to Christ during the coming trouble (Revelation 7: 9), or the fact that we are going to receive double honor and be glorified together with Jesus:

The Spirit Himself bears witness with our spirit that we are children of God, and if children, then heirs—heirs of God and joint heirs with Christ, if indeed we suffer with Him, that we may also be glorified together (Romans 8:16-17).

How about death being conquered or we will never get sick or feel pain again; that we will see our loved ones who have passed away before us?

Let's look at some promises of the millennial reign of Christ, and try to imagine what it will be like:

To comfort all who mourn, to console those who mourn in Zion, to give them beauty for ashes, the oil of joy for mourning, the garment of praise for the spirit of heaviness; that they may be called trees of righteousness, the planting of the Lord, that He may be glorified. And they shall rebuild the old ruins, they shall raise up the former desolations, and they shall repair the ruined cities, the desolations of many generations. Strangers shall stand and feed your flocks, and the sons of the foreigner shall be your plowmen and your vinedressers. But you shall be named the priests of the Lord; they shall call you the servants of our God. You shall eat the riches of the Gentiles, and in their glory you shall boast. Instead of your shame you shall have double honor, and instead of confusion they shall rejoice in their portion. Therefore in their land they shall possess double; everlasting joy shall be theirs (Isaiah 61:2-7).

So we can see it will be a good time for the people of God. We will be free to find fulfillment in meaningful work that God has ordained for us. God will bring "beauty out of our ashes." We are promised comfort and joy, and the "garment of praise for the spirit of heaviness." We will be righteous and our lives will glorify the Lord. The riches of the Gentiles will come to us. Instead of shame we will have double honor. There will be no more confusion, and we will have an abundance of love, peace, and joy.

Jesus said, "The thief does not come except to steal, and to kill, and to destroy. I have come that they may have life, and that they may have it more abundantly" (John 10:10).

So if you have not experienced the abundant life yet hang on to the end of the story.

Can you imagine people living 900 years again like in the beginning, and then on into eternity to never to feel any pain again, or get sick, or die? The word says if someone dies at 100 years old in the millennial reign, they will be considered to have died as a child (Isaiah 65:20).

All the animals will be at peace with one another as in the Garden of Eden. The wolf and the lamb shall feed together. The lion will eat grass like the bullock (Isaiah 65:25).

Satan will be bound for those 1,000 years (Revelation 20:1-2). Is it even possible to imagine a world where Satan is bound? He is the accuser of the brethren that we are putting up with now!

Our relationships will be without strife. We have seen families torn apart in our generation. All this will not exist during Jesus' reign. Family relationships will be healed: Families will be reunited.

Lift up your eyes all around, and see: They all gather together, they come to you; your sons shall come from afar, and your daughters shall be nursed at your side. Then you shall see and become radiant, and your heart shall swell with joy; because the abundance of the sea shall be turned to you, the wealth of the Gentiles shall come to you (Isaiah 60:4-5).

This will be a very good time to be alive, YOU DON'T WANT TO MISS IT! But realize there are some hard times between now and then. The world will NOT be at peace until Jesus returns and sets up His kingdom.

Looking at the joy that is set before us and God's plan for this planet will give us hope for the future.

People will not be thinking about themselves all the time, but rather how they can bless others. There would be little or no crime and children would be safe no matter where they are or who they are with. Love would reign in all situations.

Fear would be eliminated. Drug and alcohol abuse would be a thing of the past. People would love God and others with all their heart.

Medications would no longer be needed because everyone will have good health, and have the peace and joy of the Lord. Husbands and wives would live together in harmony. Divorce would be a forgotten word and everywhere we would go we would hear laughter.

So take some time and ask God to help you imagine what it will be like during His reign on earth and get that into your heart to help you endure what is coming upon us as Christians. Jesus endured the cross because of the "joy that was set before Him." If it worked for Him, it will work for us.

CHAPTER ELEVEN

OVERCOMING FEAR

IN THE NEAR FUTURE THE SPIRITUAL WAR WE are going to find ourselves fighting is guarding our heart against fear. To overcome the spirit of fear, we need to learn about God's love for us, and that we can trust Him no matter what circumstances we find ourselves in. It is recorded 365 times in the Bible to "fear not!"

For God has not given us a spirit of fear, but of power and of love and of a sound mind (II Timothy 1:7).

We have a God who is powerful and is able to deliver. He is able to give us joy and peace amidst any trouble we might be in.

Happy is the man who finds wisdom, and the man who gains understanding; for her proceeds are better than the profits of silver and her gain than fine gold. She is more precious than rubies, and all the things you may desire cannot compare with her. Length of days is in her right hand, in her left hand riches and honor. Her ways are ways of pleasantness, and all her paths are peace. She is a tree of life to those who take hold of her, and happy are all who retain her. The Lord by wisdom founded the earth; by understanding He established the heavens; by His knowledge the depths were broken up, and clouds drop down the dew. My son let them not depart from your eyes—Keep sound wisdom and discretion; so they will be life to your soul and grace to your neck. Then you will walk safely in your way, and your foot will not stumble. When you lie down, you will not be afraid; yes, you will lie down and your sleep will be sweet. Do not be afraid of sudden terror, nor of trouble from the wicked when it comes; for the Lord will be your confidence, and will keep your foot from being caught (Proverbs 3:13-26).

We have this promise from God is if we seek wisdom we will walk safely in our way and He will keep our foot from being caught. We would not be afraid and our sleep would be sweet.

Some ways we can combat our fears are:

1. Realize how much God loves us:

God loves us more than we love our own children and has the best in mind for us:

What then shall we say to these things? If God is for us, who can be against us? He who did not spare His own Son, but delivered Him up for us all, how shall He not with Him also freely give us all things? Who shall bring a charge against God's elect? It is God who justifies. Who is he who condemns? It is Christ who died, and furthermore is also risen, who is even at the right hand of God, who also makes intercession for us. Who shall separate us from the love of Christ? Shall tribulation, or distress, or persecution, or famine, or nakedness, or peril, or sword? As it is written: "For Your sake we are killed all day long; we are accounted as sheep for the slaughter." Yet in all these things we are more than conquerors through Him who loved us. For I am persuaded that neither death nor life, nor angels nor principalities nor powers, nor things present nor things to come, nor height nor depth, nor any other created thing, shall be able to separate us from the love of God which is in Christ Jesus our Lord (Romans 8:31-39).

If we really believe this we should be fearless, because if God is for us who can be against us. One plus God is a majority. We all have to die sooner or later anyway. The Bible says we will die and then the judgment; so why not die for a cause? It is better than getting old and dying of some disease. Actually, if we believe in Jesus and follow Him we never die either. Yes, our body goes in the ground, but that is not our life. To be absent from the body is to be present with the Lord (II Corinthians 5:8).

Love has been perfected among us in this: that we may have boldness in the Day of Judgment; because as He is, so are we in this world. There is no fear in love; but perfect love casts out fear, because fear involves torment. But he who fears has not been made perfect in love (1 John 4:17-18).

If we feel fear in any area of our life it is a clue that we need more of the love of God in that area. This Scripture is telling us if we have the love of God in our lives we will not have to fear when the judgments begin to fall.

God promises to provide for us. Miracles of God's provision will be experienced when they are most needed. Like the widow who gave the last of her food to Elijah, God supplied her needs during the famine (I Kings 17:8-16).

Jesus feeding the 5,000 is another example (John 6:1-13). These are recorded in the Bible to give us faith that God can provide supernaturally for us when we need it. Therefore, we do not have to take the "mark of the beast," because God has promised to provide for us when we are not able to buy or sell. There is never a recession in the kingdom of God. The main thing is to meet what is coming with love and faith. Love and faith are the currency of the kingdom.

To balance this God had Joseph store up food during seven years of plenty for the seven years of famine that was coming in the future, so it is a good idea to start storing up food and water too. Jesus had a boy's lunch to work with when He fed the 5,000.

2. Fear is a spirit and we can take it captive:

Assuredly, I say to you, whatever you bind on earth will be bound in heaven, and whatever you loose on earth will be loosed in heaven (Matthew 18:18).

Spirits can be bound in the name of Jesus. Jesus has given us the authority to bind and loose them. If you feel the spirit of fear coming on take authority over it and tell it to leave. Then seek to be filled with the Spirit of the Lord to replace it.

Death and life are in the power of the tongue, and those who love it will eat its fruit (Proverbs 18:21).

In Ephesians it says that our enemy is not flesh and blood, but that our war is against spirits.

Finally, my brethren, be strong in the Lord and in the power of His might. Put on the whole armor of God, that you may be able to stand against the wiles of the devil. For we do not wrestle against flesh and blood, but against principalities, against powers, against the rulers of the darkness of this age, against spiritual hosts of wickedness in the heavenly places. Therefore take up the whole armor of God, that you may be able to withstand in the evil day, and having done all, to stand.

Stand therefore, having girded your waist with truth, having put on the breastplate of righteousness, and having shod your feet with the preparation of the gospel of peace; above all, taking the shield of faith with which you will be able to quench all the fiery darts of the wicked one. And take the helmet of salvation, and the sword of the Spirit, which is the word of God; praying always with all prayer and supplication in the Spirit, being watchful to this end with all perseverance and supplication for all the saints— and for me, that utterance may be given to me, that I may open my mouth boldly to make known the mystery of the gospel, for which I am an ambassador in chains; that in it I may speak boldly, as I ought to speak (Ephesians 6:10-21).

These are our weapons of our warfare that we can use against the evil spirits. They are truth, righteousness, peace, faith, helmet of salvation (mind of Christ), sword of the Spirit, which is the word of God, prayer and supplication, with perseverance. Use them and then guard your mind by only letting in that which will build your faith:

3. Getting God's word and His promises into your heart: Psalm 91, the Protection Psalm, was given to us for such a time as the great tribulation and we should memorize it.

He who dwells in the secret place of the Most High shall abide under the shadow of the Almighty. I will say of the Lord, He is my refuge and my fortress; My God, in Him I will trust. Surely He shall deliver you from the snare of the fowler and from the perilous pestilence. He shall cover you with His feathers, and under His wings you shall take refuge; His truth shall be your shield and buckler. You shall not be afraid of the terror by night, nor of the arrow that flies by day, nor of the pestilence that walks in darkness, nor of the destruction that lays waste at noonday. A thousand may fall at your side, and ten thousand at your right hand; but it shall not come near you. Only with your eyes shall you look, and see the reward of the wicked. Because you have made the Lord, who is my refuge, even the Most High, your dwelling place, no evil shall befall you, nor shall any plague come near your dwelling; for He shall give His angels charge over you, to keep you in all your ways. In their hands they shall bear you up, lest you dash your foot against a stone. You shall tread upon the lion and the cobra, the young lion and the serpent you shall trample underfoot. Because he has set his love upon Me, therefore I will deliver him; I will set him on high, because he has known My name. He shall call upon Me, and I will answer him; I will be with him in trouble; I will deliver him and honor him. With long life I will satisfy him, and show him My salvation (Psalm 91).

Pray God's word until you can quote it by heart. It is meditation that takes Scripture from our head and moves it to our heart.

Application: Take some time and ask God to show you where you still could have fear. Then, do some spiritual warfare to take care of that area. Use the Scripture to overcome the enemy like Jesus did. It really does work when you quote Scripture out loud. It worked for Jesus and He is our example.

I like this Psalm too:

The Lord is my shepherd; I shall not want. He makes me to lie down in green pastures; He leads me beside the still waters. He restores my soul; He leads me in the paths of righteousness for His name's sake. Yea, though I walk through the valley of the shadow of death, I will fear no evil; for You are with me; Your rod and Your staff, they comfort me. You prepare a table before me in the presence of my enemies; You anoint my head with oil; my cup runs over. Surely goodness and mercy shall follow me all the days of my life; and I will dwell in the house of the Lord forever (Psalm 23:1-6).

Jesus can keep us in perfect peace while all the world is shaking around us. Death is only a shadow because Jesus has overcome it for us. God's goodness and mercy will follow us all our days.

Father, we pray You would deliver us from any fears that we might still have and fill us with Your Holy Spirit in the mighty name of Jesus! Amen.

CHAPTER TWELVE

CONCLUSION

I HAVE PRESENTED A CLEAR, SIMPLE, AND EASY to understand approach to end-time prophecies and the second coming of Christ. I gave some examples of how the Scriptures have been added on to say something that they don't say. This book is loaded with Scripture and the word of God because it is by hearing God's word that our faith grows.

Jesus warned us to not be deceived when He was asked about the signs of His second coming. This means deception would be rampant at this time. The second coming of Jesus is at the door, and it would be a great idea to study the Scriptures for yourself and not trust in what is being taught by many today.

These things I have written to you concerning those who try to deceive you. But the anointing which you have received from Him abides in you, and you do not need that anyone teach you; but as the same anointing teaches you concerning all things, and is true, and is not a lie, and just as it has taught you, you will abide in Him (1 John 2:26-27).

It is time for us to prepare both spiritually, mentally, and phys-ically for what we are about to experience. It is the devil's plan to confuse you and keep you off guard, so he can make you fall away, but remember what Jesus said, *"But he who endures to the end shall be saved" (Matthew 24:13).*

My brethren, count it all joy when you fall into various trials, knowing that the testing of your faith produces patience. But let patience have its perfect work, that you may be perfect and complete, lacking nothing (James 1:2-4).

The amount of patience a person possesses is the amount of love he possesses. "Love is patient, love is kind" (I Corinthians 13:4). So we are to count it all joy because the testing of our faith is what brings us into maturity. God is not the one who tests us, but He does use it to make us whole.

Blessed is the man who endures temptation; for when he has been approved, he will receive the crown of life which the Lord has promised to those who love Him (James 1:12).

Jesus didn't say it would be easy, but that it would be worth it. We have need of endurance to make it through this life and to realize this life here on earth is just a vapor and eternity is a very long time and even outside of time.

More closing exhortations:

You therefore, my son, be strong in the grace that is in Christ Jesus. And the things that you have heard from me among many witnesses, commit these to faithful men who will be able to teach others also. You therefore must endure hardship as a good soldier of Jesus Christ. No one engaged in warfare entangles himself with the affairs of this life, that he may please him who enlisted him as a soldier. And also if anyone competes in athletics, he is not crowned unless he competes according to the rules. The hardworking farmer must be first to partake of the crops. Consider what I say, and may the Lord give you understanding in all things (II Timothy 2:1-7).

This Scripture makes it clear if we are going to follow Christ it will be costly. It is impossible to please God if we are all entangled in the affairs of this life. This is a rule that says we cannot have our cake and eat it too. It is a sacrifice to live for God, but it will pay off in the end, and we know this life is but a vapor anyway.

This is a faithful saying:

For if we died with Him, we shall also live with Him. If we endure, we shall also reign with Him. If we deny Him, He also will deny us. If we are faithless, He remains faithful; He cannot deny Himself (II Timothy 2:11-13).

We can see that one of requirements of reigning with Christ throughout eternity is endurance to the end, and not to give up when things get hard and look hopeless. Usually when things look the darkest is when you are on the verge of a great breakthrough.

Jesus said, "So the last will be first, and the first last. For many are called, but few chosen" (Matthew 20:16).

But in a great house there are not only vessels of gold and silver, but also of wood and clay, some for honor and some for dishonor. Therefore if anyone cleanses himself from the latter, he will be a vessel for honor, sanctified and useful for the Master, prepared for every good work. Flee also youthful lusts; but pursue righteousness, faith, love, peace with those who call on the Lord out of a pure heart. But avoid foolish and ignorant disputes, knowing that they generate strife. And a servant of the Lord must not quarrel but be gentle to all, able to teach, patient, in humility correcting those who are in opposition, if God perhaps will grant them repentance, so that they may know the truth, and that they may come to their senses and escape the snare of the devil, having been taken captive by him to do his will (II Timothy 2:20-26).

It appears that if we are going to be a vessel of honor or dishonor is our decision. Lust of the flesh, lust of the eyes, and pride of life are of this world (I John 2:16). These are things we need to be cleansed from if we are going to be vessels of honor.

We are to seek after righteousness, humility, gentleness, faith, love, peace, and a pure heart avoiding ignorant disputes, and if we will do this we will be a true expression of our Lord Jesus, because even though He is God, He is humble and all the above.

Wash me thoroughly from my iniquity, and cleanse me from my sin (Psalm 51:2).

Create in me a clean heart, O God, and renew a steadfast spirit within me (Psalm 51:10).

We need a pure heart so we can see what God is doing. It is not more head knowledge that makes us useful to God but a clean heart.

Yes, and all who desire to live godly in Christ Jesus will suffer persecution. But evil men and impostors will grow worse and worse, deceiving and being deceived. But you must continue in the things which you have learned and been assured of, knowing from whom you have learned them, and that from childhood you have known the Holy Scriptures, which are able to make you wise for salvation through faith which is in Christ Jesus (II Timothy 3:12-15).

Jesus made it clear if the world hated Him the world would hate His followers. Satan is the god of this age and he hates Christians and Jews (II Corinthians 4:4). We are not of this world, because we are kingdom citizens. We should not be surprised when we are attacked for our faith. Our old man is dead and buried in baptism, so the attacks are against our Lord, not us. We are tempted to take attacks personally, but we don't need to if we know the truth. When we are persecuted and if we don't retaliate we are accounted worthy for the kingdom of God, and it also gives God the right to repay those who are persecuting us. "Vengeance is mine says the Lord."

I charge you therefore before God and the Lord Jesus Christ, who will judge the living and the dead at His appearing and His kingdom: Preach the word! Be ready in season and out of season. Convince, rebuke, exhort, with all longsuffering and teaching (II Timothy 4:1-2).

Our Lord wants us sharing the gospel to those who need to hear it. We heard the gospel and that is how we got saved. God chose the foolishness of the preaching of the gospel to save people from their sins. Those that don't hear the gospel and don't get saved go to hell, so it is our responsibility to get the word out. It can be uncomfortable, but we need to learn to be comfortable in uncomfortable situations. Like Paul says in one place, "Godliness with contentment is great gain," and in another place he says, "For I have learned no matter what state I am, to be content."

One thing I have learned that helps us to share the gospel is when you see a need for prayer offer to pray even if it is over the phone. Most people are happy to receive prayer and it opens the door to share Jesus with them. Also, I have learned to keep it simple; Jesus died for our sins and rose again from the grave. He loves you and wants a relationship with you. It doesn't matter what you have done He will forgive you.

Rebuke is an area most of us avoid, but we all have blind areas that we need to have people speaking into our lives. If you are one to correct others just remember to do it gently and in love. We all need to be accountable to others in the body of Christ. This is more important than most of us realize. Accountability goes a long way in overcoming strongholds. It also keeps us from drifting off and causes us to be more effective. Synergy takes effect which means more power is released when I am in fellowship with other believers.

Exhort is another word that means to encourage and we all need encouragement. Hebrews tells us to encourage one another daily (Hebrews 3:13). We reap what we sow and if we are encouraging others we will receive encouragement when we need it.

For I am already being poured out as a drink offering, and the time of my departure is at hand. I have fought the good fight, I have finished the race, I have keep the faith. Finally, there is laid up for me the crown of righteousness, which the Lord, the righteous Judge, will give to me on that Day, and not to me only but also to all who have loved His appearing (II Timothy 4:6-8).

Keep the faith and finish the race and you can say like Paul, "I have finished the race, I have kept the faith. Finally, there is laid up for me the crown of righteousness, which the Lord, the righteous Judge, will give to me on that Day."

God wants you to have a life with purpose, but without Jesus in your life, it will have very little purpose.

For I know the thoughts that I think toward you, says the Lord, thoughts of peace and not of evil, to give you a future and a hope. Then you will call upon Me and go and pray to Me, and I will listen to you. And you will seek Me and find Me, when you search for Me with all your heart (Jeremiah 29:11-13).

We are told to search for God with all of our heart and after we find Him we need to keep on following Him with all of our heart. Lukewarm Christianity doesn't work. It is a deception that we are warned about in Revelation when God rebukes the church of Laodicea (Revelation 3:14-22). So let's run the race with perseverance and know that it will be over before we know it.

I have written a Bible study guidebook to be used with this book if you are interested in doing a Bible study with a home group or Sunday school class. Included in this guidebook are many questions that can help facilitate group discussion.

My prayer is that these truths of the word of God will help you, "endure to the end." Amen

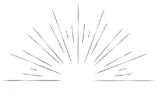

THE SEALS OF REVELATION

THE JUDGMENTS OF GOD ARE ORGANIZED INTO seven seal judgments, seven trumpet judgments, and seven bowl or vial judgments. These are recorded in the book of Revelation beginning with chapter 6 and concluding in chapter 16. Each set of judgments getting closer together and more intense like birth-pangs.

These seal judgments are the same events as the signs Jesus prophesied that would precede His second coming recorded in Matthew 24.

In chapter six of Revelation, the Lamb starts opening the seals, and we see a description of what they bring to earth, so let's compare Revelation 6 and Matthew 24:

1st Seal: Deception

Now I saw when the Lamb opened one of the seals; and I heard one of the four living creatures saying with a voice like thunder, come and see. And I looked, and behold, a white horse. He who sat on it had a bow; and a crown was given to him, and he went out conquering and to conquer (Revelation 6:1-2).

Take heed that no one deceives you. For many will come in My name, saying, 'I am the Christ,' and will deceive many (Matthew 24:4-5).

The rider has a bow without arrows and this reveals the Antichrist conquers by deception and flattery not by military might.

2nd Seal: War

When He opened the second seal, I heard the second living creature saying, Come and see. Another horse, fiery red, went out. And it was granted to the one, who sat on it to take peace from the earth, and that people should kill one another; and there was given to him a great sword (Revelation 6:3-4).

And you will hear of wars and rumors of wars. See that you are not troubled; for all these things must come to pass, but the end is not yet. For nation will rise against nation, and kingdom against kingdom (Matthew 24:6-7)

I see one seal per year being opened because there are seven years and seven seals. This would follow the birth pattern of the judgments getting closer together and more intense. So if this is true we will see these wars break out the second year of Daniel's Seventieth Week.

3rd Seal: Famine

When He opened the third seal, I heard the third living creature say, "Come and see." So I looked, and behold, a black horse, and he who sat on it had a pair of scales in his hand. And I heard a voice in the midst of the four living creatures saying, a quart of wheat for a denarius, and three quarts of barley for a denarius; and do not harm the oil and the wine (Revelation 6:5-6).

This is equivalent to a loaf of bread for a day's wages.

And there will be famines, pestilences, and earth-quakes in various places all these are the beginning of sorrows (Matthew 24:7-8).

Famine would follow the third year and wars do cause famine.

4th Seal: "Abomination of desolation" set up:

When He opened the fourth seal, I heard the voice of the fourth living creature saying, Come and see so I looked, and behold, a pale

*horse. And the name of him who sat on it was Death, and Hades fol-
lowed with him. And power was given to them over a fourth of the
earth, to kill with sword, with hunger, with death, and by the beast
(Antichrist) of the earth (Revelation 6:7-8).*

*And there will be famines, pestilences, and earth-quakes in var-
ious places all these are the beginning of sorrows (Matthew 24:7-8).*

Now we can see the seal judgments and signs of the second
coming of Jesus recorded in the gospels are the same events. Jesus
referred to the first four signs as "the beginning of sorrows."

When the fourth seal is opened the world will experience death
over one-fourth of the earth. Half way through the fourth seal the
"abomination of desolation" is set up and the great tribulation begins
and we are now half way through Daniel's Seventieth Week.

5th Seal: Christians Martyred

*When He opened the fifth seal, I saw under the altar the souls
of those who had been slain for the word of God and for the testimony which they held. And they cried with a loud voice, saying, how
long, O Lord, holy and true, until You judge and avenge our blood
on those who dwell on the earth? Then a white robe was given to
each of them; and it was said to them that they should rest a little
while longer, until both the number of their fellow servants and
their brethren, who would be killed as they were, was completed
(Revelation 6:9-11).*

*Then they will deliver you up to tribulation and kill you, and
you will be hated by all nations for My name's sake. And then many
will be offended, and will betray one another, and will hate one
another then many false prophets will rise up and deceive many
(Matthew 24:9-11).*

When the fifth seal is opened, those appointed to martyrdom will
be martyred. There will also be those who are being protected from
the Antichrist. Many will fall away from the faith at the opening of
the fifth seal because they don't understand why God is allowing

them to be persecuted. This is a contradiction to the once saved always saved belief. This will separate the wheat from the tares.

6th Seal: Cosmic Signs

I looked when He opened the sixth seal, and behold, there was a great earthquake; and the sun became black as sack-cloth of hair, and the moon became like blood. And the stars of heaven fell to the earth, as a fig tree drops its late figs when it is shaken by a mighty wind. Then the sky receded as a scroll when it is rolled up, and every mountain and island was moved out of its place. And the kings of the earth, the great men, the rich men, the commanders, the mighty men, every slave and every free man, hid themselves in the caves and in the rocks of the mountains, and said to the mountains and rocks, "Fall on us and hide us from the face of Him who sits on the throne and from the wrath of the Lamb! For the great day of His wrath has come, and who is able to stand? (Revelation 6:12-17).

Notice that God's wrath is announced at the opening of the sixth seal, but this is not the second coming, because the seals are opened chronologically and the seventh seal has not been opened yet. Therefore, there is a time delay between the opening of the sixth seal and the second coming to allow time for the seventh seal to be opened which contains the seven trumpet judgments. Jesus comes back at the "last trump" or the seventh trumpet judgment. During the sixth seal many hide themselves in the caves and the rocks and God sends fishermen and hunters after them because they have not repented.

"Behold, I will send for many fishermen," says the Lord, "and they shall fish them; and afterward I will send for many hunters, and they shall hunt them from every mountain and every hill, and out of the holes of the rocks. For My eyes are on all their ways; they are not hidden from My face, nor is their iniquity hidden from My eyes. And first I will repay double for their iniquity and their sin, because they have defiled My land; they have filled My inheritance with

the carcasses of their detestable and abominable idols" (Jeremiah
16:16-18).

Notice this judgment is directed towards those who have not
accepted Jesus. God knows who His own are and is able to keep
them safe at this time.

7th Seal: Prelude to the Seven Trumpets

*When He opened the seventh seal, there was silence in heaven
for about half an hour and I saw the seven angels who stand before
God and to them were given seven trumpets then another angel,
having a golden censer, came and stood at the altar. He was given
much incense that he should offer it with the prayers of all the saints
upon the golden altar which was before the throne. And the smoke
of the incense, with the prayers of the saints, ascended before God
from the angel's hand. Then the angel took the censer, filled it with
fire from the altar, and threw it to the earth. And there were noises,
thunder, lightning, and an earthquake. So the seven angels who had
the seven trumpets prepared themselves to sound (Revelation 8-1-6).*

Now the trumpets start to sound the last year of Daniel's
Seventieth Week.

APPENDIX B

THE TRUMPET JUDGMENTS

AT THE OPENING OF THE SEVENTH SEAL THE
trumpet judgments begin. When the seventh trumpet sounds the
earth becomes the Lord's (Revelation 10:7; 11:15)

The first six seals did not involve angels, but when the seventh seal is opened and the trumpets begin to sound angels become involved. Things on planet earth will never be the same.

1st Trumpet: Vegetation Struck

The first angel sounded: And hail and fire followed, mingled with blood, and they were thrown to the earth. And a third of the trees were burned up, and all green grass was burned up (Revelation 8:7).

Note that these judgments are tempered with God's grace to bring mankind to repentance, and to open the eyes of the blind so they can be saved.

2nd Trumpet: Seas Struck

Then the second angel sounded: And something like a great mountain burning with fire was thrown into the sea, and a third of the sea became blood. And a third of the living creatures in the sea died, and a third of the ships were destroyed (Revelation 8:8-9).

This is either an atomic bomb or an asteroid.

3rd Trumpet: Waters Struck

Then the third angel sounded: And a great star fell from heaven, burning like a torch, and it fell on a third of the rivers and on the springs of water. The name of the star is Wormwood. A third of the waters became wormwood, and many men died from the water, because it was made bitter (Revelation 8:10 -11).

Many are repenting and coming into the kingdom; because to remain an atheist at this time is to really be controlled by demons.

4th Trumpet: Heavens Struck

Then the fourth angel sounded: And a third of the sun was struck, a third of the moon, and a third of the stars, so that a third of them were darkened. A third of the day did not shine, and likewise the night And I looked, and I heard an angel flying through the midst of heaven, saying with a loud voice, Woe, woe, woe to the inhabitants of the earth, because of the remaining blasts of the trumpet of the three angels who are about to sound! (Revelation 8:12-13).

Can you imagine the darkness and weather if we only had two thirds of the sun shining during the day? This earth would really be cooling down, not getting warmer.

5th Trumpet: Locusts from the Bottomless Pit

Then the fifth angel sounded: And I saw a star fallen from heaven to the earth. To him was given the key to the bottomless pit. And he opened the bottomless pit, and smoke arose out of the pit like the smoke of a great furnace. So the sun and the air were darkened because of the smoke of the pit. Then out of the smoke locusts came upon the earth. And to them was given power, as the scorpions of the earth have power. They were commanded not to harm the grass of the earth, or any green thing, or any tree, but only those men who do not have the seal of God on their foreheads. And they were not given authority to kill them, but to torment them for five months. Their torment was like the torment of a scorpion when it strikes a man. In those days men will seek death and will not find it; they will desire to die, and death will flee from them. The shape of the locusts was like horses prepared for battle. On their heads were crowns of something like gold, and their faces were like the faces of men They had hair like women's hair, and their teeth were like lions' teeth And they had breastplates like breastplates of iron, and the sound of their wings was like the sound of chariots with many horses running into battle. They had tails like scorpions, and there were stings in their tails. Their power was to hurt men five months. And they had as king over them the angel of the bottomless pit, whose name in Hebrew is Abaddon, but in Greek he has the name Apollyon. One woe is past. Behold, still two more woes are coming after these things (Revelation 9:1-12).

We see the 144,000 Israelites that are sealed are here during the fifth trumpet judgment proclaiming the "day of vengeance of God" (Isaiah 61:2b), and while they are being protected others are being tormented. This really shows who has power over death. They are those who are trying to die because of the pain and are not able to. Sometimes it is hard to see God's mercy in all of this, but if many are coming into the kingdom and being saved from hell at this time; this would be God's mercy even if it doesn't look like it from a natural perspective. God sees the beginning and the end and if He can save someone with some temporary suffering from an eternity of suffering He will do that. All suffering comes from the devil, but God does turn it around and uses it for good.

For when Your judgments are in the earth, The inhabitants of the world will learn righteousness (Isaiah 26:9b).

Multitudes, multitudes in the valley of decision! For the day of the Lord is near in the valley of decision the sun and moon will grow dark, and the stars will diminish their brightness the Lord also will roar from Zion, and utter His voice from Jerusalem; the heavens and earth will shake; but the Lord will be a shelter for His people, and the strength of the children of Israel (Joel 3:14-16).

6th Trumpet: The Angels from the Euphrates

Then the sixth angel sounded: And I heard a voice from the four horns of the golden altar which is before God, saying to the sixth angel who had the trumpet, release the four angels who are bound at the great river Euphrates. So the four angels, who had been prepared for the hour and day and month and year, were released to kill a third of mankind. Now the number of the army of the horsemen was two hundred million; I heard the number of them. And thus I saw the horses in the vision: those who sat on them had breastplates of fiery red, hyacinth blue, and sulfur yellow; and the heads of the horses were like the heads of lions; and out of their mouths came fire, smoke, and brimstone. By these three plagues a third of mankind was killed-by the fire and the smoke and the brimstone which came out of their mouths. For their power is in their mouth and in their tails; for their tails are like serpents, having heads; and with them they do harm. But the rest of mankind, who were not killed by these plagues, did not repent of the works of their hands, that they should not worship demons, and idols of gold, silver, brass, stone, and wood, which can neither see nor hear nor walk. And they did not repent of their murders or their sorceries or their sexual immorality or their thefts (Revelation 9:13-21).

Multitudes have been saved during the fifth trumpet by Christian evangelists. One-third of mankind is killed in this sixth trumpet judgment. You can see times are getting pretty tough to say the least. It is obvious to mankind that God's judgments are falling just like they were foretold in the book of Revelation. Everyone is without excuse from here on out. Those who have not repented by now will not repent in the future either, and they will go on to experience the bowl judgments that are coming next after the seventh trumpet sounds.

7th Trumpet: The Lord Returns

The seventh angel sounded: And there were loud voices in heaven saying, the kingdoms of this world have become the kingdoms of our

Lord and of His Christ, and He shall reign forever and ever! And the twenty-four elders who sat before God on their thrones fell on their faces and worshiped God, saying: We give You thanks, O Lord God Almighty, The One who is and who was, and who is to come, Because You have taken Your great power and reigned. The nations were angry, and Your wrath has come, And the time of the dead, that they should be judged, And that You should reward Your servants the prophets and the saints, And those who fear Your name, small and great, And should destroy those who destroy the earth. Then the temple of God was opened in heaven, and the ark of His covenant was seen in His temple. And there were lightning, noises, thunder, an earthquake, and great hail (Revelation 11:15-19).

The "wrath of God" is announced at the opening of the sixth seal and now it is actually come at the seventh trumpet when Jesus returns.

Let's bring this all together. All the seals and trumpets are released in chronological order. These judgments are tempered by God's mercy because He is giving man more time to repent. This is God's harvest time and His laborers go forth brining a multitude to Jesus. This is when Jesus sees His reward of His suffering and sacrifice on the cross. The sign of the Son of Man appears when the "last trump," is sounded and we will see Jesus coming in the clouds. He resurrects His chosen ones and then pours out the bowl judgments Himself which is the "fierceness of the wrath of Almighty God.".

Now I saw heaven opened, and behold, a white horse. And He who sat on him was called Faithful and True, and in righteousness He judges and makes war His eyes were like a flame of fire, and on His head were many crowns. He had a name written that no one knew except Himself. He was clothed with a robe dipped in blood, and His name is called the word of God. And the armies in heaven, clothed in fine linen, white and clean, followed Him on white horses. Now out of His mouth goes a sharp sword, that with it He should strike the nations. And He Himself will rule them with a rod of iron. He Himself treads the winepress of the fierceness and

ND TIME PROPHECY MADE SIMPLE

wrath of Almighty God. And He has on His robe and on His thigh a name written:

KING OF KINGS AND LORD OF LORDS (Revelation 19:11-16)

Those who were deceived by the Antichrist and took the "mark of the beast" will now experience the bowl judgments. The elect are with Jesus now and will watch the destruction of the wicked.

Only with your eyes shall you look, and see the reward of the wicked (Psalm 91:8).

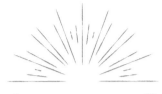

THE BOWL JUDGMENTS

THE BOOK OF REVELATION IS THE REVELATION of Jesus Christ. He came the first time as a lamb. He is coming the second time as a lion. He came the first time as the Savior. He is coming the second time as a king and judge. The bowl judgments are the "great winepress of the wrath of God" (Revelation 14:19). They are hell come to earth so that the kingdom of heaven can come. Jesus is a forgiving and merciful God to those who accept Him, but on the other hand, He is a God of vengeance for those who have rejected Him. God has promised in His word that everything that can be shaken will be shaken, so that everything that opposes love will be shaken out of the earth. Believers in Christ are in His kingdom and cannot be shaken. If you are not in His kingdom as of yet, may I suggest that you become a kingdom citizen.

Jesus said, "For these are the days of vengeance, that all things which were written may be fulfilled" (Luke 21:22).

God is jealous, and the Lord avenges; The Lord avenges and is furious. The Lord will take vengeance on His adversaries, and He reserves wrath for His enemies (Nahum 1:2).

Why do the nations rage and the people plot a vain thing? The kings of the earth set themselves, and the rulers take counsel together, against the Lord and against His Anointed, saying, "Let us break their bonds in pieces and cast away their cords from us." He who sits in the heavens shall laugh; the Lord shall hold them in derision. Then He shall speak to them in His wrath, and distress them in His deep displeasure (Psalm 2:1-5).

We can see that not everyone is happy about Jesus coming back to rule, and those kings that Satan has in power at the time try to stop it, and they will incur the "wrath of God".

All those who have refused the salvation that God offers through His son Jesus and have taken the "mark of the beast" will experience the bowl judgments, so whatever you do don't take the "mark of the beast" Those that take the mark are the ones who were deceived by the signs and wonders that the False Prophet performed. They saw these miracles not realizing the Satan can perform miracles, so he deceived them into thinking the Antichrist was God.

Then I saw another sign in heaven, great and marvelous: seven angels having the seven last plagues, for in them the "wrath of God" is complete (Revelation 15:1).

1st Bowl: Loathsome Sores

The first angel went and poured out his bowl upon the earth, and a foul and loathsome sore came upon the men who had the mark of the beast and those who worshiped his image (Revelation 16:2).

This Scripture makes it clear that these judgments are for those who received the "mark of the beast." It is too late for them to repent and God had even sent an angel to share the gospel to give them a chance to repent, but they wouldn't. These are the tares that the enemy sowed amongst the wheat. (Matthew 13:24-30).

2nd Bowl: Sea turns to Blood

The second angel poured out his bowl on the sea, and it became blood as of a dead man; and every living creature in the sea died (Revelation 16:3).

Wow, can you imagine all of the sea being blood and everything in it dying and washing up on shore.

3rd Bowl: Waters turn to Blood

The third angel poured out his bowl on the rivers and springs of water, and they became blood. And I heard the angel of the waters saying: You are righteous, O Lord, the One who is and who was and who is to be, because You have judged these things. For they have shed the blood of saints and prophets, and You have given them blood to drink. For it is their just due. I heard another from the altar saying, Even so, Lord God Almighty (Revelation 16:4-7).

God is a just God. We reap what we sow (Galatians 6:7). The Antichrist has martyred many followers of Jesus, not realizing he was causing his own doom. Now there is no water to drink. "Unless these days are shortened no flesh would be saved." The Antichrist is now reaping what he has sown.

4th Bowl: Men are Scorched

The fourth angel poured out his bowl on the sun, and power was given to him to scorch men with fire Men were scorched with great heat, and they blasphemed the name of God who has power over these plagues; and they did not repent and give Him glory (Revelation 16:8-9).

Still there is no repentance. These are beyond salvation. In the book of Isaiah it says the sun will become seven times brighter and the moon as bright as the sun when the Lord heals His people (Isaiah 30:26). So the destruction of this present world system and age is the manifestation of our salvation.

There will be on every high mountain and on every high hill rivers and streams of waters, in the day of the great slaughter, when the towers fall. Moreover the light of the moon will be as the light of the sun, and the light of the sun will be sevenfold, as the light of seven days, in the day that the Lord binds up the bruise of His people and heals the stroke of their wound (Isaiah 30:25-26).

5th Bowl: Darkness and Pain

The fifth angel poured out his bowl on the throne of the beast, and his kingdom became full of darkness; and they gnawed their tongues because of the pain. They blasphemed the God of heaven because of their pains and their sores, and did not repent of their deeds (Revelation 16:10-11).

Jesus promises that there would be gnashing of teeth in darkness. Their god was Satan and just like the Antichrist blasphemed God they do too. This is not a pretty site, and we really need to start praying for our love ones to come to Jesus so they don't have to go through this pain. This is a horrible site to say the least.

6th Bowl: Euphrates Dried Up

The sixth angel poured out his bowl on the great river Euphrates, and its water was dried up, so that the way of the kings from the east might be prepared. And I saw three unclean spirits like frogs coming out of the mouth of the dragon, out of the mouth of the beast, and out of the mouth of the false prophet. For they are spirits of demons, performing signs, which go out to the kings of the earth and of the whole world, to gather them to the battle of that great day of God Almighty. Behold, I am coming as a thief. Blessed is he who watches, and keeps his garments, lest he walks naked and they see his shame. And they gathered them together to the place called in Hebrew, Armageddon (Revelation 16:12-16).

These are the kings talked about in Psalm two that try to stop Jesus. I mentioned in the chapter on the feasts of the Lord that the return of Jesus takes place over several days. The kings of the earth see Jesus coming in a military campaign up through Jordan on His way to the Mount of Olives (Isaiah 63:1-6; Habakkuk 3). They surround Jerusalem to meet Him only to meet their waterloo at the battle of Armageddon.

7th Bowl: The Earth Utterly Shaken

The last and seventh angel poured out his bowl into the air, and a loud voice came out of the temple of heaven, from the throne, saying, it is done! And there were noises and thunder and lightning; and there was a great earthquake, such a mighty and great earthquake as had not occurred since men were on the earth. Now the great city was divided into three parts, and the cities of the Nations fell. And great Babylon was remembered before God, to give her the cup of the wine of the fierceness of His wrath. Then every island fled away, and the mountains were not found. And great hail from heaven fell upon men, each hailstone about the weight of a talent. Men blasphemed God because of the plague of the hail, since that plague was exceedingly great (Revelation 16:17-20).

This earthquake must be at least a 10.0 on the rector scale. When it says all the mountains and islands are not found, it must be talking about all the governments of this present time, because we will still have mountains and islands during the millennial reign.

We see everything that man has created without God is coming down. It is like an old shopping center that needs renovated. Here comes the wrecking crew and they take everything down, and everything is rebuilt to the new owners delight:

And they shall rebuild the old ruins, they shall raise up the former desolations, and they shall repair the ruined cities, the desolations of many generations (Isaiah 61:4).

So when Jesus comes back and sets up the millennial kingdom you will not be sitting on a cloud playing a harp, because you will be helping rebuild the ruined cities and the desolations of many generations.

The End

GLOSSARY[5]

ANTICHRIST, THE — a False Prophet and evil being who will set himself up against Christ and the people of God in the last days before the second coming. He is referred to as the Beast out of the sea in the book of Revelation.

ARMAGEDDON (mountain of Megiddo) the site of the final battle of this age in which God intervenes to destroy the armies of Satan and to cast Satan into the bottomless pit (Rev. 16:16).

CHRONOLOGICAL — means in sequence, something following one after another in a sequence.

DANIEL'S SEVENTIETH WEEK — a seven year period of tribulation just prior to the second coming of Jesus Christ (Daniel 9:27).

ESCHATOLOGY — the study of what will happen when all things are consummated at the end of history, particularly centering on the event known as the second coming of Christ.

FEASTS AND FESTIVALS — the holy convocations, the regular assemblies of the people of Israel for worship of the Lord. These

---

[5] Nelson, Thomas, 1986, *Nelson's New Illustrated Bible Dictionary*

feast days were types and shadows (rehearsals) of events that were in the future.

GREAT COMMISSION — given by Jesus to make disciples of all nations. And Jesus came and spoke to them, saying, "All authority has been given to Me in heaven and on earth. Go therefore and make disciples of all the nations, baptizing them in the name of the Father and of the Son and of the Holy Spirit, teaching them to observe all things that I have commanded you; and lo, I am with you always, even to the end of the age" Amen. (Matt. 28:18-20).

LAMB OF GOD — a phrase used by John the Baptist to describe Jesus (John 1:29, 36). John publicly identified Jesus as "the Lamb of God who takes away the sin of the world!" Elsewhere in the New Testament Jesus is called a lamb (Acts 8:32; 1 Pet. 1:19; Rev. 5:6). The Book of Revelation speaks of Jesus as a lamb 28 times.

MARK OF THE BEAST — referred to in the book of Revelation and given out by the Antichrist and if you will not take it you cannot buy or sell (Rev. 13:16-17). Most likely a computer chip placed on your right hand or forehead.

MARRIAGE SUPPER OF THE LAMB — The celebration marriage supper the Lord will have with His bride upon His return. The party is with Jesus not with the devil in hell. That is a lie that the devil wants you to believe.

MESSIAH [meh SIGH uh] (anointed one) — the one anointed by God and empowered by God's spirit to deliver His people and establish His kingdom. In Jewish thought, the Messiah would be the king of the Jews, a political leader who would defeat their enemies and bring in a golden era of peace and prosperity. In Christian thought, the term Messiah refers to Jesus' role as a spiritual deliverer, setting His people free from sin and death.

MID -TRIBULATION RAPTURE VIEW — believes the Church will be raptured at the mid-point of Daniel's Seventieth Week.

MILLENNIAL REIGN OF CHRIST — a thousand year period that Jesus will reign over the earth after His second coming. It will be time of transition from the temporal to the eternal.

NISAN — the name given after the Captivity to Abib, the first month of the Jewish sacred year (Esth. 3:7).

POST-TRIBULATION RAPTURE VIEW — believes the Church will be resurrected at the end of Daniel's Seventieth Week at the "last trump."

PRE-TRIBULATION RAPTURE VIEW — believes in a secret coming of Jesus and the Church will be raptured before Daniel's Seventieth Week.

PRE-WRATH RAPTURE — believes the rapture takes place at the opening of the sixth seal two thirds of the way through Daniel's Seventieth Week.

SECOND COMING — Christ's future return to the earth at the end of the present age. Although the Bible explicitly speaks of Christ's appearance as a "second time," the phrase "second coming" occurs nowhere in the New Testament. Many passages, however, speak of His return. In fact, in the New Testament alone it is referred to over 300 times. The night before His crucifixion, Jesus told His apostles that He would return (John 14:3). When Jesus ascended into heaven, two angels appeared to His followers, saying that He would return in the same manner as they had seen Him go (Acts 1:11). The New Testament is filled with expectancy of His coming, even as Christians should be today.

SHADOW —the Bible also uses the word to contrast the Jewish and Christian periods. The Jewish regulations, rituals, and rules are "a shadow of things to come, but the substance is of Christ" (Col 2:16-17).

TISHREI — the seventh month of the religious year in the Jewish calendar, also called Ethanim (1 Kin. 8:2).

TRIBULATION, THE GREAT — a short but intense period of distress and suffering at the end of time. The exact phrase, "the great tribulation," is found only once in the Bible (Rev. 7:14). The great tribulation is to be distinguished from the General Tribulation a believer faces in the world (Matt.13:21; John 16:33; Acts 14:22). It is also to be distinguished from God's specific wrath upon the unbelieving world at the end of the age (Mark 13:24; Rom. 2:5–10; 2 Thess. 1:6). The great tribulation fulfills Daniel's prophecies (Daniel 7–12). It prophets (Mark 13:22) when natural disasters will occur throughout the world. It takes place in the last 3½ years of Daniel's Seventieth Week.